Hill Walking

and

Scrambling

Hill Walking
and
Scrambling

STEVE ASHTON

The Crowood Press

First published in 1987 by
THE CROWOOD PRESS
Ramsbury, Marlborough
Wiltshire SN8 2HE

© Steve Ashton 1987

Reprinted 1988

British Library Cataloguing in Publication Data

Ashton, Steve
    Hill walking and scrambling.
    1.   Walking — Great Britain
    I.   Title
    796.5'22   GV199.44.G7
    ISBN 0-949284-58-X

Dedicated to Tony, for the very best of mountain days

Acknowledgements
The author acknowledges the help of the following: The
Technical Committee of the British Mountaineering
Council for their thought-provoking discussions on the
choice and use of equipment; Dr Anthony S. G. Jones of
the Ogwen Valley Mountain Rescue Organisation for
advice on the rescue emergency checklists; Dr Ieuan
W. Jones for advice on the first-aid checklist; and Tony
Ashton for invaluable assistance with the manuscript and
photographs.
Fig 81 courtesy of Lyon Equipment; Figs 136 and 138
courtesy of Minolta (UK) Limited; Fig 137 courtesy
of Olympus Optical Company. All other photographs
and line illustrations by the author.

Typeset by Alacrity Phototypesetters, Banwell Castle,
Weston-super-Mare, Avon
Printed in Great Britain at the University Printing House, Oxford

Contents

Preface

Mountains symbolise permanence – or so it seems when viewing them through the distorting hourglass of our own time. They are not perturbed by the progression of days and seasons: darkness comes and goes, and the snow falls and melts away. The greatest change is the slow accumulation of small stones at their feet. By comparison our movements among them are frantic. There is so little time: darkness shuts us out; winter slows us down; and our legs and lungs are hard pressed to fulfil even the most meagre ambitions.

No single thread binds those who walk in the mountains. Some see it as healthy recreation for Sunday afternoons, others as a way of life, but none fail to be moved by the encounter.

Sometimes there are false starts. My own initiation at the age of eleven proved traumatic. One of thirty school children on a snow-covered Lakeland fell, inexpertly led and clutching for survival to a wind-shredded plastic mac, my life was in peril before it had really begun. That spike of early experience must have survived the steamroller of adolescence. Years later, when circumstance had brought me to the hills again, I found myself pricked by an urge to recreate the drama – if not the misery – of that first climb. As a result I was drawn towards rock climbing and Alpinism – realms of self-inflicted trauma.

My approach to mountains has mellowed with time. In stripping away the veneer of danger I have uncovered an altogether quieter side. Now ordinary things seen and done add colour and texture to what was once, and superficially still is, the wearying process of ascending hills by putting one foot above the other. It has taken me twenty years to experience what others scoop up at first dip.

All this is of no significance but for the fact that it has led, however indirectly, to this book being written in the way that it has. Every handbook has at its source a pool of knowledge filled up over the years by passing luminaries. This one is no exception and I acknowledge the debt. However, the emphasis and omissions of a book depend on the author's own predilections, and if that is thought to be an abuse of the fund I must take the blame.

The one regret in writing this book, preoccupied as it is with skills and learning, is that it will fail to communicate properly what is most captivating about mountains – their capacity to instil in us the primitive significance of being alive.

HILL WALKING

Fig 1   On the Snowdon Ranger path, Snowdon.

1 The Mountains of Britain

The mountains of Britain are small, but we are proud of them. It is often the prospect of adventure in hill walking which draws us away from our firesides, not simply the desire for altitude.

The mountains are grouped within well-defined upland areas situated predominantly in the north and west of the mainland, and around the coasts of Ireland. Some lie within designated National Parks. Of these the Lake District is by far the most popular, the classic juxtaposition of high fell and tree-lined lake having captivated generations of country lovers. Scotland and North Wales appeal with more rugged countenances, while the Peak District and Pennines delight with an unexpected mixture of bleak moorland tops and bubbling dales. Each mountain area in each season offers unique experiences to the walker and scrambler; from the arctic vehemence of a Scottish blizzard, to the timeless peace of a Pennine moor.

All major summits are accessible in summer to the experienced walker. Geological good fortune – the work of ice caps, glaciers and post-glacial erosion – has produced shapely hills among which gentle grass slopes and plunging cliffs sit side by side. Difficulties may be sought or avoided at will. Broad paths, gouged by thousands of boots, score the gentler flanks of popular peaks, while those who seek solitude will find it in the untrodden land between. In good weather there is no uncertainty and little adventure to these outings, although the exercise is undoubtedly healthy and the views invariably fine. Others will find

excitement on the rocks of a knife-edged ridge or in the green depths of a gill. Rock scrambling such as this bridges the gap between neighbouring realms of walking and climbing, combining the freedom of one with the exhilaration of the other.

Restrictions on access are mostly confined to valley pastureland, although even here a network of rights of way and courtesy footpaths forms links to the high ground. Once beyond fenced land, there exists in most areas an agreement between farmers and walkers for free access. On the whole the arrangement works very well indeed, although from time to time normally good relations are strained by inconsiderate behaviour from one side or the other.

Accommodation presents little difficulty. Most upland areas are populated by small communities which extract livelihoods from the land and from tourism. It follows that campsites, barns, bunkhouses, hostels and bed and breakfast rooms abound.

What follows is a very brief introduction to the three main hill walking areas of Britain: Scotland, the Lake District and Wales. Unfortunately the mountains of Ireland, though offering equivalent opportunities, are for most walkers as inaccessible as the European Alps. Mountain literature is well served by lavishly illustrated descriptions of each of these areas, and the bibliography has some suggestions for further reading. In addition to these mountainous regions are those where upland walking of a more gentle character may be enjoyed, particularly in the Pennines and the South

West. But it is from within that central core – with the prospect of rock scrambling and winter expeditions ahead – that hill walking enlists its lifelong devotees.

SCOTLAND

The Scottish mountains excite unusual fervour. This has something to do with their scale and dominating appearance, but also with that sense of isolation peculiar to northern latitudes. You feel its influence strengthen as you travel northwards, leaving behind the cities and flatlands of the south.

Sporting interest in the Highlands before the First World War was largely confined to game fishing and shooting: pursuits enjoyed by the affluent few with the facility for travel, a penchant for the outdoor life, and sufficient spare time for its proper indulgence. With them came men from the professions who sought in the Scottish mountains a solitude and grandeur which, they felt, had been stripped from their home hills of the Lake District and Wales. Meanwhile the local inhabitants, in common with other hill people, had little time or inclination to seek further hardship in their lives by climbing mountains.

Times have changed. No longer the preserve of the favoured few, the Scottish mountains are now within reasonable

Fig 2   Blackmount from the Rannoch Moor.

Fig 3 Glencoe – Bauchaille Etive Beag (left) and Beinn Fhada from Am Bodach.

travelling distance of most of the population centres. Motorways, cheap coach fares and hired minibuses have made the long-weekend visit a reality. Not that growing familiarity has diminished their stature at all. These peaks are generally higher and more remote than their counterparts further south; it follows that the scope for hill walking is proportionately greater. However, only those with the fitness and experience to match will benefit. Long distances, ill-defined paths and the frequency of snowfalls make hard and exacting work of walking the Scottish mountains. The rewards, though, are tremendous.

Altitude, climate and – of all things – a vindictive species of wildlife limit the best summer walking months to just May, June and September. On the highest ground full winter conditions may extend from November through to May, while the dreaded midges nibble away much of the enjoyment during July and August. For these reasons winter walking is practised more often here than is the norm further south.

Although it is usual to talk collectively about the Scottish mountains, distribution and geological differences divide them into quite distinct areas: the Northern Highlands, mysterious and remote; the Cairngorms, bleak and unforgiving; the Islands

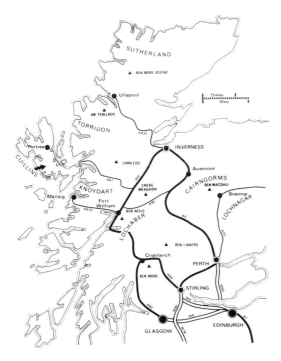

Fig 4 Access routes to the main mountain areas in Scotland.

and West Coast, craggy and sculptured. *Fig 4* shows their location, while numerous maps, guidebooks and inspirational narratives describe their individual characters.

Well-known bases include Glenbrittle (Skye), Glencoe (Ben Nevis and Glencoe) and Aviemore (Cairngorms). However, because of the distances involved – and bearing in mind the relative infrequency of visits – it is common practice to tour a number of areas in an attempt to net as wide a variety of experience as possible.

LAKE DISTRICT

If the mountains of Scotland are thought of as inaccessible and imposing, then those of the Lake District are intimate and obliging.

This is due in part to their relative proximity to the towns of the industrial north, and to a long tradition of Sunday or weekend outings. The local people bear the annual crush of visitors with remarkable stoicism.

Simply as a place to tour – let alone walk – the Lake District is delightful in every respect; each turn reveals some new and subtle arrangement of trees and lakes and bracken-covered fellside. The walks themselves weave natural lines among the rockwalled basins of high corries; or along the slender, interconnecting fingers of the high ridge crests. Beautiful and intricate, this is the spiritual home of the hill walker.

Lower in altitude and latitude than Scotland and greatly influenced by warm air blowing inland from the sea, the Lake District has a summer walking season which typically extends from mid-April through to mid-November. Unfortunately the weather itself is no better; an average summer day is characterised by impenetrable cloud cover on the fells and ceaseless

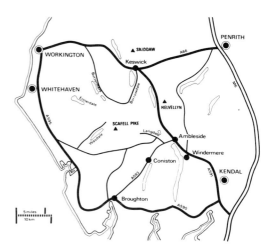

Fig 5 Access routes to the main valley bases in the Lake District.

Fig 6   Langdale.

light rain in the valleys. Some days are much worse, few are better. In recompense there is more scope here to salvage something from the day, contriving a worthwhile short walk from among the lattice-work of paths on the lower fells.

Geographically more compact than the Scottish mountains, the high fells are clustered in a series of small, neighbouring groups separated by lake-filled hollows. Valley bases serve the most popular of them; Wasdale, Borrowdale and Langdale being among the more convenient and well known (*Fig 5*). Excellent maps and a plethora of guidebooks (the Wainwright series being outstanding) detail each nook and cranny with loving care. Although

precious little remains which has not already been trodden or recorded, the thrill of personal discovery survives intact in this enchanted garden.

WALES

Exploring Wales means uncovering tracts of Scotland, stumbling upon little oases of the Lake District, and, of course, experiencing a great deal that is uniquely its own.

The mountains of Wales have never attained the popularity of those in the Lake District. During early visits the hills seem to lack the coherence and identity of Lakeland fells and are difficult to get to grips with. In

13

Fig 7   *Cader Idris – Pen y Gadair and the view west towards Barmouth.*

Fig 8   *Snowdon group from Moel Siabod.*

time, though, when their secrets have finally been teased from the more remote cwms, a new and lasting appreciation is formed.

Once again the predominant climatic influence is the sea: winters are mild, summers wet. In most years the tops are clear of snow from April to November, but it is especially important to be aware of their precise condition during these change-over months. The difficulty of many of the most popular paths increases dramatically when under snow or ice. This is due to the ruggedness of terrain in central areas. A typical path on to the Glyders or Snowdon will ascend a rocky ridge or find a devious way through a barrier of crags. Encountered during the descent, perhaps in failing light, such a passage may present formidable difficulties when iced.

Central Snowdonia attracts most visitors. Each weekend sees hundreds of walkers setting off from Ogwen or Pen y Pass to climb the Glyders, Carneddau or Snowdon. Peace and quiet seem hard to find, and yet there are places among these hills, especially in the ranges further east and south, where not half a dozen people will venture all summer.

One of the great delights is to link summit with summit along the intervening ridges. By this means it is possible to cover twenty miles – over perhaps five or six hills – expending little extra effort beyond the initial gruelling ascent to the first summit. Classic ridgewalks combined in this way include such famous outings as the Snowdon Horseshoe and the Idwal Skyline, as well as lesser known but equally enjoyable traverses

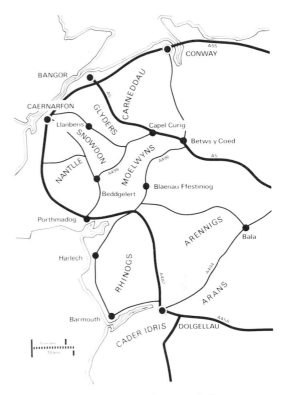

Fig 9   Access routes to the main hill groups in North Wales.

along the Moelwyns and Rhinogs.

Capel Curig, Llanberis and Beddgelert serve as bases for the main hill groups (*Fig 9*), each having adequate facilities for long or short stays. However, in common with most mountain areas public transport is at best irregular. As in the Lake District, Ordnance Survey maps offer comprehensive information on topographical detail and major paths, but here there is much less choice among guidebooks and illustrated narratives; hidden qualities are apparently difficult to describe.

15

2 Basic Equipment

In hill walking the quality or success of the outcome rarely depends on the performance of equipment. If there *is* to be a struggle, it will be engaged with will-power not the contents of a rucksack. Initially, when early enthusiasm overcomes all discomfort almost anything will do. But before long you start to realise that sore feet and a wet shirt add nothing to your enjoyment. It is then time to reappraise your equipment. First, consider the following general guidelines.

Get clear in your mind what function these early purchases will serve. Will they be stopgaps until you can afford something better; or are they to form the basic core of your equipment, later to be expanded in line with ambitions? If the latter is the case you will be able to justify investment in top quality equipment. On the other hand, too much forward planning could invite costly mistakes with overspecified items. In practice, some sort of balance seems wise, and this is reflected in the advice given below.

Almost without exception it pays to buy from a specialist retailer. Most large towns have one, and their whereabouts are listed in the equipment suppliers directories in the outdoor magazines (*see* bibliography). Here at least you will have some guarantee that the equipment on show is suitable for your purposes. Fashionable imitations in high street stores often prove inadequate when exposed to the rigours of the mountain. The guidelines that follow will help you decide what items you require. The next step is to seek specific advice from the retailer on which particular brand would best suit your needs and budget.

Having agonised over the initial choice – and backed your decision with hard cash – it makes sense to protect the investment by careful use and storage. Materials used in outdoor equipment survive rough usage remarkably well, but there is no defence against maltreatment. Footwear is most obviously at risk.

Finally, but without relinquishing your rights as a consumer, guard against disappointment by adopting a realistic attitude towards expected durability and performance. Although manufacturers like to entice with boldly worded advertisements, in practice *all* outdoor equipment ultimately breaks down: proofings disintegrate; the soles of boots wear out; seams come apart – none of it will last forever.

FOOTWEAR *(Figs 10 to 13)*

The choice of footwear takes priority over any other equipment buying decision – it is that important. Obvious things to get right are size, comfort, quality and price. But the first question to settle in your own mind is one of use and suitability. For instance, boots designed purely for summer trail walking will not be very satisfactory on the mountain tops in winter (and vice versa). A *good* boot, therefore, is one which fits your foot and fits your ambition. But be honest, or you'll find yourself hoisting an awful lot of unnecessary weight up the summer hillsides.

Trainers, running shoes and other ultra-lightweight footwear have limited

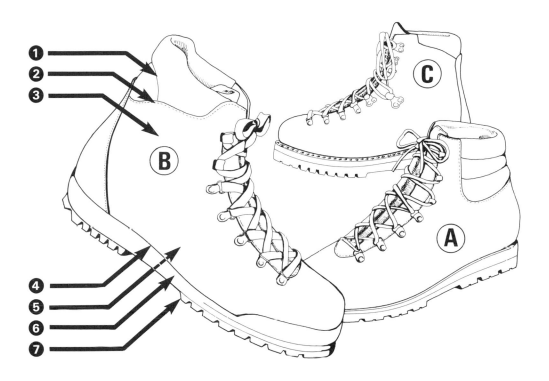

Category	A	B	C
	(summer walking)	(walk/scramble)	(winter)
1 Ankle cuff	deep	medium	short
2 Ankle	low	medium	high
3 Upper	supple	firm	stiff
4 Welt	bonded	bonded	stitched
5 Stiffener	flexible	firm	stiff
6 Midsole	EVA foam	'monobloc' rubber	leather
7 Sole	light	medium	heavy

Fig 10   The main differences between light, medium and heavy duty walking boots.

application, principally trail walks and competitive events. At the other end of the scale, Alpine or winter climbing boots (identified by plastic uppers and inflexible soles) have valuable advantages in winter, as they are warm and are easily fitted with crampons, but are otherwise heavy, cumbersome and expensive.

That narrows the choice to footwear which is reasonably light and flexible, yet which promises adequate grip and protection when walking or scrambling. Within this category the choice is subdivided in the following way: boots designed for summer

17

Choosing Boots

Try this method of obtaining correct fit:

1. Wearing just one pair of thick socks, begin with boots one full size larger than your normal shoe size.

2. While standing upright, and with the laces fully undone, push your foot forward until your toes press against the front of the boot. Now bend your leg forward slightly and slide a finger, turned sideways, into the gap revealed between your heel and the rear of the boot. It should just fill this space. If not then try the next size.

3. Lace up the boot (tightly, so that your heel is forced back into its proper position) and apply your full weight. Your foot should spread to fill the width of the boot – without pinching, but with no room to spare.

4. Now bend forward so that the sole flexes. Provided you haven't fallen over, check that your toes fail to touch the front of the boot; your heel lifts away from the insole by no more than a couple of millimetres (but if it does check that the laces have not slackened); and that the natural 'crease' which inevitably forms across the top of the boot does not dig into your toes.

5. If necessary add a thin sock to achieve ideal fit.

6. Repeat the procedure with at least one other pair of comparable boots before making a decision on which offers the most comfortable and secure fit.

7. Ask the retailer if you may wear the boots at home for a few hours on approval.

Fig 11   Lightweight Vibram Sole. A light and durable sole despite the shallow tread.

Fig 12   The Scarpa Trionic Sole, which retains the deep tread of early Vibram-type soles. Note the treaded cutaway heel to ease strain from repeated impact of the heel.

Fig 13   The Meindl Sole Unit utilises a foam shock-absorbing wedge to ease strain from heel impact. Note the padded ankle cuff to prevent bruising.

use only; boots ideally suited for winter but usable in summer; and boots which are a compromise of the previous two. This is a very difficult area of choice and one which keen walkers frequently resolve by purchasing two pairs – a light boot for summer walks and scrambles and a heavier one for winter.

Summer boots are typified by flexible soles, shallow tread, medium height ankles, and soft uppers. The priorities of design are comfort and lightness. By comparison winter boots are generally heavier and less immediately comfortable, featuring stiff soles, deep tread, and high ankles. The priorities here are warmth, resistance to water penetration, and good security on

Boot Care

All boots, no matter how comfortable initially, require breaking-in to the shape of your feet. Begin by wearing new boots around the house for a few days, and then on progressively longer walks. If the bottoms of your feet blister, try wearing an extra sock to fill up space. If the tops of your toes blister, try wearing a thinner sock or removing the contoured footbed. If your heel rubs, try lacing the boot tighter, especially at the top. If your ankle bruises, try leaving the topmost hooks unlaced. Finally, if all else fails, part-exchange the boots for something more comfortable and put it down to experience.

Observe the manufacturer's recommendations regarding treatment of uppers. Some require regular treatment with boot wax or cream, others occasional buffing with shoe polish. But all boots benefit by having traces of mud washed off after use, followed by unhurried drying in a well-ventilated place away from direct heat. Boots dried near a fire or on top of a radiator will take offence and shrivel up inside.

Monitor tread wear and have the boots resoled before damage spreads to the vulnerable midsole area. The cost of repair will be approximately one-third of the current price of the boots. Most retailers can make the arrangements. Avoid high street shoe repair shops who seem to have a propensity for glue and staples.

snow (with or without crampons). Obviously the 'compromise' boots function at various stages between, depending on design emphasis.

CLOTHING

Successful hill clothing meets our requirements with just the right combination of function and flair. It must do the job of keeping us warm and dry, but not entirely at the expense of freedom of movement, lightness, comfort, durability, and care convenience.

Basic clothing, carefully chosen, lays the foundation of a complete and versatile system capable of weathering both sunshine and storms. With that aim very firmly in mind, there seems little point in squandering your initial budget on an exotic purchase like a down jacket. Instead you will be looking towards the adaptability of a *layered* set of clothes. This often means choosing each item of clothing to fulfil just one requirement: that of being warm, windproof or waterproof. This way each layer is more likely to perform its task well. *Fig 14* shows one way to build up an adaptable, multi-layer clothing system; summarised below are its constituent parts.

Stockings

The choice in stockings is between long or short, thick or thin, standard or loop-stitch,

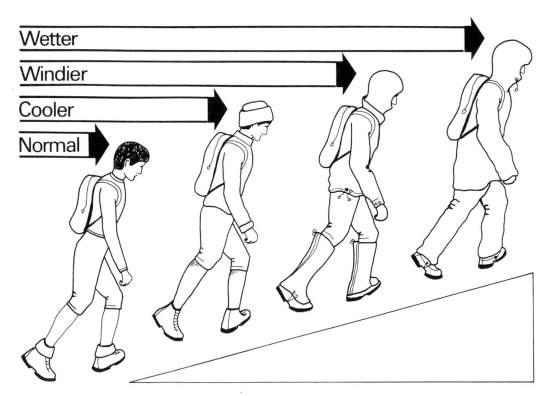

Wetter
Windier
Cooler
Normal

Fig 14   Each layer of clothing has a specific task to perform. The layer system is more efficient and adaptable than the use of a single multi-functional garment.

wool or nylon. For reasons of both comfort and durability the most popular are long, thick, loop-stitch stockings in a wool/nylon mixture (usually 70 per cent wool, 30 per cent nylon). An old pair of football or hockey socks is an adequate stopgap; if necessary a pair of short, cheaper socks can be worn over the top in order to fill up space left by oversized boots.

Underwear

In this context the main role of underwear is to stabilise temperature at the skin surface. Ordinary nylon or cotton shirts are conspicuously poor in this respect. Of little warmth value in themselves, the material also inhibits removal of sweat. As a consequence you quickly feel cold when resting after heavy exertion. So-called *thermal* underwear is the best answer. There are numerous materials in use, each claiming a special advantage over its competitors. In practice the differences between brands are marginal when compared to their mutual superiority over cotton T-shirts. Old, close-fitting sportswear (such as a rugby shirt) could be used as an interim measure.

Long johns, inner gloves and thermal Balaclavas are useful in very cold conditions, but I shall discuss these in more detail in the chapter on winter equipment.

Legwear

Knee-length breeches in stretch nylon fabrics or windproof polycotton have been popular for some years. Although there is no reason why full length trousers made from similar materials should not be used, denim jeans and other types of casual trousers lack the substance to cope with the combined wet and cold of poor weather.

Equipment Checklist (summer)

Boots
Long socks
Short socks
Breeches/trousers
Undershirt
Midwear (pullover)
Windproof
Waterproof
Hat
Gloves

Spare pullover
Spare socks/gloves
Map
Compass
Torch
Whistle
Food/drink
First-aid kit
Survival bag
Rucksack

Qualities to look for in breeches and trousers are: a close but unrestrictive fit, high degree of windproofness, adequate but not excessive warmth, fast drying capability, lightness, and care convenience. The size and location of pockets and reinforcing patches are of secondary importance.

Shorts are often worn in high summer (despite the risk of sunburn), but it is very important to carry alternative legwear in case of sudden changes in weather or temperature.

Midwear

This category of clothing describes the layer traditionally occupied by a wool pullover. Its function is to insulate the trunk and arms from the cold, maintaining efficiency even when dampened by sweat or rain. Wool does this job very well, but it tends to absorb water and become heavy and is also slow to dry. Modern midwear materials, such as *pile* and *fleece*, imitate the fibrous and bulky nature of wool, while at the same time introducing properties of low absorption and high durability.

Ironically the most important property of a midwear garment proves not to be its fabric type but its design, and unfortunately a great deal of 'specialist' midwear is designed with more emphasis on fashion than function. Whether styled as a jacket, shirt or pullover, good basic design features to look for are: close but unrestrictive fit; good air sealing at wrists, waist and collar; and facility for high arm movement (i.e. without causing waist hem to lift up).

Outerwear *(Figs 15 to 17)*

The function of the outer layer of clothing is to protect the insulating layers from the cooling effects of wind and rain: it forms a barrier. By nature a waterproof jacket is also windproof (for all practical purposes), although the reverse is not always true.

There are many excellent and reasonably priced waterproof fabrics on the market which are based on polyurethane or neoprene proofed nylon. Unfortunately these conventional waterproof barriers also resist the passage of water *vapour*. Evaporated sweat, having nowhere to go, condenses on the inside of the waterproof shell, soaking back into the midwear layer and undermining its ability to insulate. This wetting from within is infinitely preferable to the potential soaking from without, but that is little consolation when all you want to do is protect against a cold wind on a dry

Fig 15   *An efficient mountain jacket. Note the detachable hood with stiffened peak, high collar, self-locking drawcords, generous cut at the shoulders, press-studded storm flap, waist drawcord, bellows pockets with flaps, and Velcro-fastened cuffs.*

day.. One answer is to wear a windproof jacket or overshirt in water-repellent (showerproof) nylon, polycotton, or Ventile, and to carry a lightweight waterproof top in readiness for heavy downpours.

An alternative solution to the waterproof/condensation dilemma is furnished by 'breathable' waterproof materials, such as *Gore-Tex* and its competitors. Fully effective against wind and rain, their proofing structure allows molecules of water vapour (evaporated sweat) to permeate the fabric

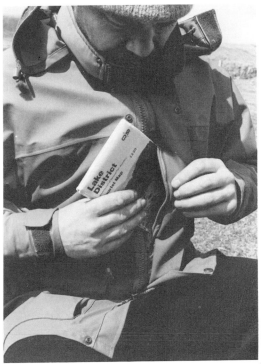

Fig 16   Two-way zips promote free leg movement when ascending steep slopes.

Fig 17   A storm flap protects the map pocket without unduly restricting access.

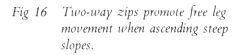

and escape to the outside air. Some fabrics are more efficient in this respect than others, but all will relieve condensation to a degree. These materials are usually much more expensive (and yet no more durable) than conventionally proofed nylons of equivalent weight; you pay for comfort.

Once again, successful performance of outerwear on the hill (as opposed to on the test bench) depends more on garment design than fabric structure. There are too many individual features to list, but as a general principle the jacket must be capable of offering its protection with minimum hindrance to normal movement. When choosing a jacket pay particular attention to the

means of closure at front, neck, face and wrists. Note that self-locking toggles, Velcro tabs, press-studs and plastic two-way zips are quick and easy to operate in rough weather. Conversely, buttons, cord ties and fine metal zips can be thoroughly frustrating.

There is conflicting advice on waterproof overtrousers. Some people regard them as essential, whereas others happily go without. Certainly, the protection offered is to a less vulnerable part of the body (most of which is in any case already protected by the jacket), and on steep ground they definitely inhibit free leg movement. But for level walking during torrential rain they

23

are none the less worth having. An acceptable compromise might be a light and inexpensive pair which will happily reside in the rucksack until required for just such an occasion.

Headwear

Consideration of this small but extremely important item of hill clothing is all too frequently neglected. In fact, heat losses from the head account for a substantial proportion of the total: up to a third from an otherwise properly clothed body. Mountain top conditions are such that a warm hat may be needed even in midsummer. Bob-caps or ski hats are adequate at most times, whereas Balaclavas are better for winter.

Gloves

You might need gloves at *any* time of year. Wool or its synthetic equivalents are probably best; unlike leather they retain some warmth value even when saturated. Ordinary wool gloves are inexpensive (and will double as inner gloves for winter). Check for long cuffs and unrestrictive fit at the base of the fingers. Handwear for very cold weather will be discussed in more detail in Chapter 10.

EMERGENCY EQUIPMENT

Estimating the standard of emergency provision is one of the more difficult equipment decisions to make: too little leaves you vulnerable; too much adds to weight and therefore discomfort. It is impractical to cater for every eventuality, so you must decide which are most likely to occur. Listed in no particular order they might be: delay, exhaustion, bad weather, benightment, minor injury, major injury and ill-health. An emergency will often develop progressively – a catalogue of disaster – so that, for example, bad weather may cause a route finding error which in turn leads to delay, benightment and ultimately exhaustion. This sorry tale conveniently identifies equipment that could be carried as a precaution.

Spare Clothing

The temptation here is to carry either too much or nothing at all. In summer just one spare item of midwear (for example a wool pullover) is sufficient. Spare socks will revive wet feet and if necessary could substitute for mitts.

Route Finding and Signalling

Map and compass appear superfluous in familiar hills during good weather, but to leave them behind is to invite trouble. When mist descends without warning your hill may no longer be quite so familiar. I shall discuss this in more detail in the following chapters.

A torch and plastic whistle should be carried as signalling devices to alert rescue services (*see* Chapter 15). The torch is also useful for map reading and path finding as daylight fades. The merits of various types are discussed in Chapter 10.

Food

After a good breakfast it is physically possible to enjoy a full and energetic day on the hills without eating again until your return. However, this makes no allowance for extra demands placed on stamina by unforeseen delay. Quite apart from the boost to energy, food administered at times of stress can give a tremendous psychological uplift. Sandwiches (with moist fillings), fruit and biscuits are fine for ordinary rations; whereas emergency reserves are best compiled from easily consumed items such as chocolate, dried fruit, nuts and sweets.

Drink

Hot flasks are a heavy luxury in all seasons but the depths of winter, as are litre bottles of fizzy drink or fruit juice. Instead, and with a little care and foresight, it is usually possible to drink from natural sources as you go along. A small, sealable, plastic cup will allow stream water to be collected for the intervening dry sections.

During very dry weather, or when following ridges, you will have no option but to carry a filled water bottle. Plastic inevitably splits so it is worth investing in a metal bottle. The half litre size should be adequate for one person on an average walk.

First Aid

There is no point kitting up for injuries and ailments you are unable to diagnose or treat. A practical approach to a first-aid kit (discussed in more detail in Chapter 15) is to cater for the two extremes of injury: minor but annoying (blisters, sunburn, grazes); and major but treatable (mainly severe bleeding). The middle ground of multiple small cuts and minor fractures can usually be dealt with by improvisation – at least until more expert help arrives.

Survival Bag

This preserves body heat in someone immobilised by injury or benightment. The basic type is simply a heavy duty polythene bag of approximate dimensions 2.4m × 1.2m (8ft × 4ft), coloured bright orange for ease of location by rescuers. Reflective foil bags, 'space' blankets and thin gauge polythene bags have no advantage over the standard survival bag (apart from their light weight) and are much more likely to disintegrate in high winds or on rough ground. Bags in Gore-Tex are more comfortable but very expensive. Designed for planned bivouacs, their capacity for retaining heat – in a survival sense – is less efficient (i.e. some warm air is 'breathed' out through the fabric walls).

RUCKSACKS *(Figs 18 to 22)*

You will now need somewhere to put all this equipment. Forget the big backpacks – they offer no tangible advantage in carrying the typical weights incurred on day walks – and concentrate instead on the ranges of daysacks, of which there are many.

Major Considerations

Some forward planning is wise here to avoid later redundancy.

Capacity

Decide first of all if you will be carrying equipment for people other than yourself (a couple or family group may wish to cut costs by taking turns at carrying a single rucksack). If so, then for year-round use you could be looking for a capacity of between

Fig 18   Chest and waist straps aid stability on rough ground.

Fig 19   Quick-release buckles are convenient and simple to adjust.

45 and 55 litres – and all the better if distributed among a number of sewn-on pockets.

Assuming only personal equipment is carried – and this is much the best arrangement – a capacity of about 25 litres will be adequate for summer hill walking and scrambling. A minimum of 35 litres is more useful in winter. If you fully intend to go out in winter, although they are a little more expensive, you may as well buy one of these slightly larger daysacks from the start. The added weight and inconvenience when carried partially empty in summer will be negligible.

Comfort

Having decided on capacity, and given that the quality of material and manufacture is acceptable (go to a specialist retailer to help ensure this), the next most important consideration is comfort.

Shouldering the display sample is a complete waste of time: *all* rucksacks feel comfortable when full of foam blocks and polystyrene chips. Instead, get an empty rucksack and weight it by an amount 50 per cent more than your normal load. Now try it.

Things to be wary of are: narrow, short or stiff shoulder pads that dig into the shoulders, underarm or neck; inflexible

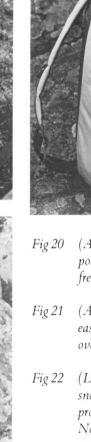

Fig 20 (*Above left*) *An exterior map pocket is useful for small items in frequent use.*

Fig 21 (*Above right*) *A zipped lid gives easy access but is unusable with oversized loads.*

Fig 22 (*Left*) *A conventional lid. The snow-flap and elasticated lid protect loads in bad weather. Note the axe attachment loops on this winter daysack.*

back frames that happen not to suit your physique; and waistbelts that are positioned either too high or too low.

Fittings

Convenience of fittings is the next consideration. Some people like to stow small items in exterior side or lid pockets, whereas others prefer the clean lines of a single compartment. A lot depends on where you like to carry small items such as map, gloves, food and so on.

Some rucksacks are closed with semi-circular zips, others more conventionally by draw cords and lids. The zip models are neat and stable for summer walking and scrambling, but often sacrifice convenient fittings for the sake of a clean-looking profile. If the sack is to be used in winter it makes sense to choose one that offers an efficient means of sealing the main compartment, as well as a facility for ice-axe attachment.

Finally, find yourself a large plastic bag to use as a waterproof liner for the rucksack; the stitch lines will leak even if the panel fabric does not.

3 Route Planning

In competitive sports the fixture list dictates when and where the players will next take part. In hill walking, apart from a club's informal meets list or loose arrangements made among friends, we can bring the whole episode from inception to execution within our personal control. Although giving us a great deal of freedom, this lack of direction may just as easily fragment ambitions. When faced with so many alternatives the simplest solution is often to make no choice at all. To combat this some people use guidebooks and their lists of peaks to help formulate plans. This 'summit-bagging' approach to hill walking frequently attracts criticism, but few can resist the orderliness of it all. With some it becomes an obsession. For instance, there are many walkers who harbour secret (and not so secret) desires to ascend the 500 or so Scottish summits above 3,000ft listed in *Munro's Tables*.

MAPS AND GUIDEBOOKS

Maps and guidebooks are a source of fireside inspiration as well as being of practical help on the mountain. All mountain areas are minutely detailed in maps of various scales, while the best walks in each are painstakingly described by innumerable local guidebooks.

Guidebooks

Guidebooks fall into one of three categories. Most common is a 'lefts-and-rights' type of descriptive text supported by occasional sketch maps or photo-diagrams. However useful in the field, most of these make dull reading by the fireside. Large format glossy or 'coffee table' books make good this deficiency with lavish illustrations and entertaining essays. Their role is essentially inspirational. Slotted somewhere between these two are the illustrated guides which seek both to inspire and to guide (of which the best example is the Wainwright series of pictorial guides to the Lake District). Eminently collectable, such guidebook companions are perhaps the most useful of all. The bibliography makes some suggestions.

Walks guides are most helpful when anticipating a visit to a new area. At this stage you simply require suggestions for reliable and uncomplicated routes by which to sample new surroundings. The danger thereafter lies in treating the guidebook as your Bible, blinding yourself to the many possibilities which exist beyond its scope. Having got to know an area, a better source of inspiration will be the map itself. But first you will need to familiarise yourself with its set of common symbols and conventions. Only then will you be able to pre-visualise the topography and terrain your route will cross – the most useful skill of all at the route planning stage.

Maps for Mountains

Early interest in map reading is too easily suffocated under a blanket of tedious arithmetic and fiddly compass exercises. The answer is to take things one stage at a time. The first stage asks for nothing more taxing than ordinary mental arithmetic and a little imagination.

Two scales of map are commonly used in hill walking: the standard 1:50,000 (a few maps still use the old one-inch-to-one-mile scale which is slightly smaller) and the more detailed 1:25,000. Almost all are published by the Ordnance Survey. Some popular mountain regions are served by special editions of the 1:25,000 scale maps. These deviate from the usual boundaries in order to include the area of greatest interest on a single sheet. This saves having to buy three or four maps. Another attractive feature of these maps is that they emphasise places of special interest to visitors: footpaths, camp-sites, youth hostels, mountain rescue bases and so on.

Terrain is more easily visualised at the 1:50,000 scale, so these maps are the most useful at the preliminary planning stage. Although they contain sufficient detail for following popular walks, only the larger scale (1:25,000) maps will show the important nuances of an intricate route. There is merit in having both – at least for favourite areas.

When first looking at a mountain map, the most obvious aids to visualisation are shades and colour: green for woods, blue for lakes, dark grey for cliffs, and so on. Some of the best maps in this respect are those in Alpine areas, where there is great complexity of mountain and glacial terrain. Unfortunately some British mountain maps accord no special status to high ground. Some will argue that colour and shade obscure important detail, but without it a general interpretation is more difficult to achieve. In their absence, contour lines are your best aid to visualisation.

Map Conventions

Contour Lines (Figs 23 & 24)

Contour lines add a third dimension to the map. With their aid it is possible to build up an image of the topography: its peaks and hollows, ridges and valleys. Contour lines connect points of equal altitude and are normally traced out at ten metre height intervals. Bunching of lines betrays the presence of a steep slope, whereas a scarcity indicates level ground or a gentle gradient.

With practice, study of the curvature and distribution of contour lines invokes a mental image of the landscape. For example, contour lines grouped as a series of concentric circles (in the manner of growth rings exposed in a tree trunk) will represent a conical hill. But equally they could represent a funnel-like hollow! To avoid ambiguity the altitudes of contour lines are printed on the map at convenient intervals. Nevertheless, the risk of wrongly interpreting a ridge as a valley (or vice versa) perpetually haunts even the most experienced of map readers.

Interpreting contour lines is initially one of the more frustrating aspects of map reading. It is like trying to make sense from a plate of spaghetti. Like a picture puzzle, some people 'see it' straight away, whereas others remain baffled. A useful aid is to imagine that the mountain has been compiled from layered sheets. In this analogy, contour lines simply mark the edges of each sheet.

Scale

Map scales are normally described as a simple ratio (e.g. 1:50,000), but such numbers are not very helpful when attempt-

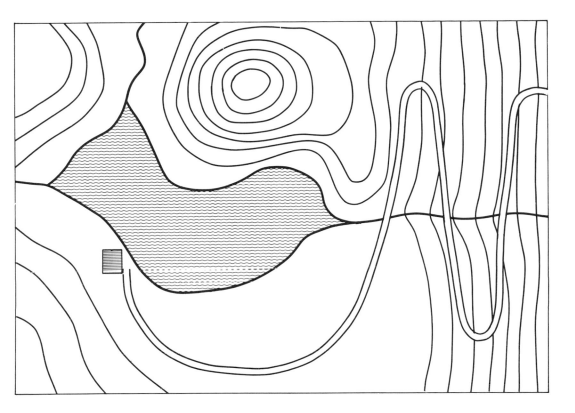

Fig 23   Contour lines indicate the shape and steepness of mountain features, but can be difficult to interpret.

ing to estimate walking distance. A quick calculation reveals that 2cm on a 1:50,000 map represents 1km on the ground (4cm to 1km in the 1:25,000 scale). It is easy to see from this that the 1:25,000 scale will give us much greater detail than the 1:50,000, but that to cover the same area we would need to buy four times as many maps. It hardly needs saying that before making any calculations it is wise to check which scale of map is being used!

A length of string knotted at 2cm (or 4cm) intervals is a useful planning aid. After tracing out the line of the route, it is a simple matter to count the knots and convert to kilometres. Although the method takes no account of extra distances hidden within deviations and undulations, the result will serve as a first approximation.

Conventional Signs

A key to symbols accompanies each map; it is usually found on the rear cover. Many symbols (including those which distinguish between lighthouses and lightships or spired and spireless churches) are entirely superfluous to our needs – though much beloved of scout masters and geography teachers. That said, failure to distinguish between a footpath and a parish boundary – some of which take perverse delight in descending

31

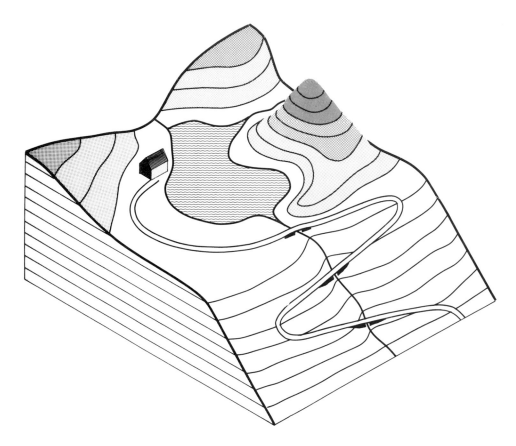

Fig 24   3-D visualisation of contour lines. Imagine the landscape
compiled from layers.

vertical cliffs – could land you in deep trouble. Otherwise, important symbols to recognise for the planning stage are those which represent the various kinds of terrain and vegetation: scree, boulders, cliffs, marsh, scrub, and so on.

The Grid (Fig 25)

The grid, part of a nationwide system, is a network of lines overprinted on each map. It divides the area into a series of numbered squares, the sides of which – irrespective of the map scale – represent one kilometre. Any point in Britain may be uniquely described (to within a few tens of metres) by quoting its grid reference and the map sheet number. The system has clear advantages when arranging a rendezvous – emergency or otherwise – and is frequently used by guidebook writers to confirm the location of important features or turning

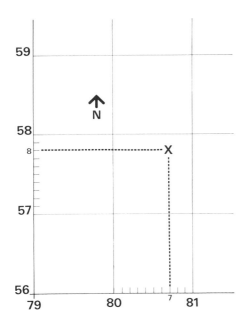

Fig 25   The six-figure grid reference for point X is GR: 807 578.

points in the path.

A six-figure grid reference is usual. This is compiled by reading off first the east/west position of the point, then its north/south position. Precisely how to arrive at the answer is easier to demonstrate than describe (*Fig 25*). Because the reference consists only of numbers, there is always a danger of confusing the two sets. Various mnemonics have been devised to help us to remember the correct order. Here are a few of them:

You must go along the hall before going up the stairs.
E for eastings comes before N for northings.
H for horizontal comes before V for vertical.

ROUTE PLANNING (*Fig 26*)

Given that the walk will be limited either by the number of daylight hours or by our capacity or inclination to keep going, some indication of its likely duration would be a very valuable piece of information. That is one thing the map does not tell us – or at least not directly. What we do have is an estimate of distance (courtesy of the knotted string) and of height gain (from the spot heights and contours). A simple formula (Naismith's) relates these variables:

Allow one hour for every 5km travelled, plus half an hour for every 300m height gained.

Naturally this formula takes no account of time lost to resting or diversions. Other factors to be taken into account include: nature of terrain (are the ridges broad and gentle, or knife-edged and rocky?); type of vegetation (might the valleys be choked with deep heather?); and prevailing weather (will the ridges be exposed to strong winds?). Chapter 14 has more to say about this.

The most valuable aspect of route planning is the freedom of choice it grants. Otherwise, by forever following popular opinion or the guide writer it could be that you are failing to indulge your own interests to the full. Moreover, not everyone agrees on what makes a great day: some find inspiration in rugged crests, others in intricate corries. Now the map lets you choose.

Logistics

Ironically the most daunting problem faced during a long weekend away may be encountered not on the mountain but down in

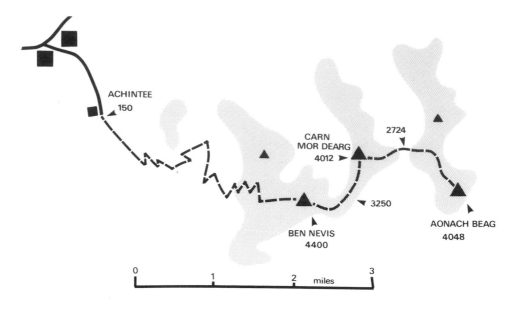

ACHINTEE
150

CARN
MOR DEARG
4012 ►

2724

BEN NEVIS
4400

3250

AONACH BEAG
4048

0   1   2   miles   3

*Fig 26   Route planning using Naismith's Rule. The equivalent
formula for use with 1-inch Tourist Maps is: allow an
hour for every 3 miles travelled, plus half an hour for
every 1,000 feet of height gained. In this example the
ambitious ascent from Achintee Farm, via Ben Nevis
and Carn Mor Dearg, to Aonach Beag should take
about 6 hours (8 miles plus 6,200 feet of accumulated
ascent). To this figure will be added a time allowance
for rests and a supplement for the rocky ascent to Carn
Mor Dearg, say 8 hours in all (plus the descent time).
The result is very approximate but nevertheless useful
for assessing the feasibility of route plans.*

the valley. It is astonishing how rapidly a
day can dissolve into chaos, losing hours of
precious daylight. If walking is to have
priority – rather than campcraft or touring
or gourmet eating – then positive steps must
be taken to simplify basic arrangements. In
particular it is worth aiming to be self-
sufficient in food; to be conveniently based
for early starts; and to be independent with
regard to transport. Then all will be well –
provided, of course, your companion shares
your enthusiasm and sense of purpose.

Logistics also have a bearing on the
choice of route itself. Public transport in
mountain areas can only be described as

rattlingly skeletal – and that's on the good
days! So unless the party has access to two
cars or you are prepared to end the day with
a long road walk, it might be best to choose
a route which conveniently returns you to
your starting point.

Weather Forecasts

Understanding how and why the weather
affects your route is of great importance,
summer or winter (Chapter 13 describes the
principles). Meanwhile, a great deal can be
learned from the regular media forecasts.

Irrespective of source, these general

34

points apply when interpreting forecasts:

- Upland weather is invariably worse than that of surrounding coastal or low-lying areas.
- Hilltop conditions are cooler, windier and wetter than those experienced at lower levels.
- Weather at altitude can deteriorate rapidly, sometimes with little warning.

With these points in mind, special allowances must be made when interpreting any of the following types of forecast.

Newspapers

Newspaper forecasts are already out of date by the time you see them. Information given is accordingly of the most general nature. Some papers include a weather map; provided you can interpret the symbols, these give some indication of the dominant trend.

Recorded Weather Forecasts

Scotland: Glasgow (041248) 5757
Lake District: Windermere (09662) 5151
Snowdonia: Llanberis (0286) 870120

Television

Consistent advances in meteorology over recent years – particularly in satellite observation – have greatly improved the reliability of these forecasts. A national forecast often proves to be more informative than a regional one, perhaps because the prediction is made within the context of an overall weather pattern. As a general rule, mountain top temperatures will be between 5 and 10 degrees (C) lower than forecast (*see* Chapter 13 for an explanation

of this phenomenon), whereas precipitation will be at least one stage more advanced (i.e. 'blustery showers' will actually arrive as squalls, and so on).

Radio

Most radio forecasts are scarcely more helpful than those in the newspapers, although they do have the advantage of being more up to date. One exception is the shipping forecast which is potentially quite useful, particularly since most of Britain's mountainous regions lie close to the west coast, so their weather is dominated by westerlies. Most of the relevant information is given in terms of pressure changes and wind strengths (enabling synoptic charts to be drawn up – a pointless exercise unless you have the ability to interpret the results). Those still clueless as to what 'Vikings' and 'Pharoahs' have got to do with the weather will make more sense out of the general forecast which is broadcast immediately afterwards.

Recorded Forecasts

The telephone directory and code book list numbers which may be dialled for detailed local forecasts, some of which include a prediction of mountain weather and ground conditions. These are especially useful the evening and morning before a walk.

Written Forecasts

Local forecasts may sometimes be found pinned on National Park bulletin boards and in climbing shops. This information is likely to be detailed and directly relevant, possibly including predictions of temperature, cloud level and wind speed.

4 On the Mountain

FINAL PREPARATION

It sometimes happens that motivation falters at the last hurdle. But how, with the rucksack packed and the route planned, is it possible to feel mentally unprepared? A common thread among the many possible explanations (besides those invented to conceal a shameful laziness) is the inevitable disruption to routine caused by a weekend away: too much alcohol; a restless night; an unconventional breakfast.

It would be ludicrous to propose a regime of mental and physical preparation – a pattern of pre-match behaviour – for an activity as athletically unrefined as walking. But it is true none the less that enjoyment of the day can depend on its stable beginnings. If for you that means a good night's sleep followed by a simple breakfast of coffee and cornflakes, then so be it. Unless you have the constitution to assimilate it, feeding a hangover with the traditional hill walker's breakfast of a huge mixed grill mopped up with four slices of fried bread is guaranteed to bring you to your knees within the hour.

Last Minute Checks

A final equipment check before leaving will often reveal an embarrassing oversight: no bootlaces, for instance. This is also a good time to make sure someone has packed the communal items: compass, first-aid kit, and so on.

Ideally this is also the time to get an update on the weather forecast, or to sniff the air and judge for yourself whether or not yesterday's prediction was accurate. It could be that some feature promised by the weather chart, for example a cold front, has in fact arrived earlier than expected, suggesting a change of plan.

The usual textbook advice will urge you to deposit with a responsible person a note of your intended route and expected time of return. Apart from improving your chances of survival if something goes wrong, this is in deference to the mountain rescue teams who must come to look for you. For a large group this procedure is of unquestionable value, but it can place severe restrictions on a small party. Not only is there a temptation to complete the route against all odds, but also a danger of forgetting to cancel the message if ultimately you do decide to modify your route and descend to a different location. With this in mind it is sometimes better to leave word of only your most general intentions.

DURING THE WALK

Pace and Rhythm

The exhortation for pace and rhythm when hill walking drags like a ball and chain on youthful enthusiasm. Plodding along all day, head down, never stopping or tiring – where is the fun in that? But that isn't it at all. Finding pace and rhythm really means plugging-in to the environment. Once we become aware of its gradient and texture, our progress through the day becomes much

Fig 27 Ascent of Carnedd Llewelyn, North Wales.

more fluent and lively. It is the difference between a yacht and a power boat. It has something to do with placing the soles of our boots deliberately; shortening and lengthening our stride as the gradient varies; choosing a zigzag path to ascend the steepest slopes; and regulating our breathing. Pace and rhythm develop naturally; scientific analysis kills them stone-dead.

Use of Equipment

Proper use of equipment comes less naturally to us. Time after time we find ourselves toiling up steep slopes while fully wrapped and sweating, only to remove layers of clothing on reaching the top in order to cool off while resting. Two minutes later, not fully recovered but complaining of the cold, we must move on again to keep warm. In our hurry we have failed to appreciate how the body and our clothing work together to regulate temperature. On reflection what we should be doing is precisely the opposite: removing clothing when active to minimise sweating and adding it again later to prevent undue heat loss while resting. It takes discipline to stop part of the way up a slope to remove a pullover instead of gamely suffering and 'getting it over with'.

The parallel case is our reluctance to stop and put on extra clothes or waterproofs when the weather turns cold or showery. Perversely this results from our subconscious reluctance to upset the precious walking rhythm which will have developed during the day. The solution is to make stopping easy. If waterproofs are accessible at the top of the rucksack and buckles and closure cords are easy to operate there is less of an excuse to keep trudging bravely on.

The phenomenon shows itself again in our resistance to adjust footwear. Socks and boot uppers tend to bed down as the day progresses, and blisters or rubbed skin are a certainty unless laces are tightened at intervals.

It could be the same mental affliction which tempts us to save our food and drink for the windswept summit, there to gulp and stuff it all down in a half-hour binge that leaves us feeling both ill and cold. Only in retrospect is it obvious that we might have benefited from some of that energy and psychological uplift lower down the mountain.

Access

Access to hill country, lying within a National Park or otherwise, is not guaranteed by right. It often happens that access is permitted simply because the landowner has no reason to object. Paths used like this for many years are eventually designated public rights of way. These are accorded special distinction on most OS maps (but not in Scotland, where the legal position of rights of way is less clear).

Some access paths have been negotiated between farmers and bodies such as the national park authorities in order to transport walkers across lower pastureland with a minimum of disturbance to crops and livestock. These are clearly waymarked and well furnished with stiles and gates. It is in everyone's interest to keep to them.

On reaching high ground there is usually little restriction on access, although once again this situation owes more to courtesy than to law. If challenged to leave, and if reasoned discussion breaks down, the best course of action may be to return as directed and then discreetly seek out a nearby alternative. Unreasonable restrictions on access can be reported to the British Mountaineering Council.

Temporary restrictions on access are occasionally installed to prevent the spread of animal disease or to protect wildlife during a vulnerable season in its life cycle. At such times notices will be found displayed in prominent places in the hope of enlisting the co-operation of walkers.

Conservation and Consideration

Much of the incidental interest we find while walking – evidence of hill farming, rare plants, wild animals – thrives in its own right and quite outside the momentary attention we are able to devote to it. In fact, our arrival on the scene frequently gives rise to conflicts of interest; difficulties which if they are to be resolved require patience and understanding from everyone concerned. Acrimony evaporates in the face of mutual respect.

Considerate parking is a good way to begin, taking care not to block tractor turning bays and field entries. The same consideration is called for when passing through fields and pastures, and that means closing gates and resisting short cuts over fences or across cultivated fields. If no obvious means of crossing farmland presents itself then you are probably in the wrong place.

Most upland areas are grazed by sheep, so dogs must be kept under strict control – on a lead if necessary. No dog can be trusted during lambing time (mid-winter to late spring), and it is wise to leave them at home.

Wild animals cling precariously to life in the barren upland environment. Given a fair chance they will survive, but not if repeatedly disturbed by our casual curiosity. The continued existence of certain plants hangs by an equally slender thread; remember that it is the photograph, not the pressed exhibit, which is the more faithful record.

Sometimes it is we who suffer from the thoughtless actions of others – be they individuals such as farmers or corporate bodies such as the Forestry Commission. What unites us against them on these occasions is that eyesores like post and wire fencing or block conifer plantations shatter the precious illusion of wilderness. By the same token our wilderness is also threatened from within; the pollution of noise, litter,

Fig 28   *Remedial work on this popular
Lake District path hopes to correct
unsightly erosion scars.*

eroded paths, and waymarking cairns is of
our own making. Organisations such as the
British Mountaineering Council, Ramblers'
Association, National Trust, and the
national park authorities variously work –
often amid controversy – to resist exploita-
tion of upland areas and to put right the
damage. There is no instant cure for any of
it, but in the meantime we can do much
simply by doing nothing. We can enter and
leave our 'wilderness' as we would a
cathedral.

Route Finding

Most hill walks follow routes so well
marked that on a clear day the map is
redundant. With the objective in view and a
good path underfoot, surely all that remains
is to follow each twist and turn to the
summit. Not quite: mountain paths con-
verge and diverge at frequent intervals; *up*
paths are sometimes different from the *down*
paths; sheep tracks start here and there but
lead nowhere in particular; and even major
paths lose themselves from time to time
among boulder fields or broad expanses of
grass. Suddenly you are a pioneer.

Route finding skills operate at one of
three levels: general orientation, local
manoeuvring and immediate positioning.

General Orientation

Success at this level appears to depend on a
subconscious analysis of such things as sun
position, wind direction and stream flow.
We just *know* when we are homing in on
our destination. Are we always right? We
like to think so, but when put to the test we
discover that our sense of direction is much
too erratic to be entirely relied upon during
poor visibility. Hence the need for a map
and compass.

Local Manoeuvring

An experienced eye will survey a complex
hillside and at once discern the best route to
follow: dodging outcrops; crossing streams
at their shallowest; avoiding bogs and scree
and uncooperative boulders. But how, by
what mental process? The feeling for a good
line comes only after a long exposure to
route finding challenges – and the consequences of bad judgements. There is much
to ponder while completing the remainder
of a walk with wet feet or bruised ankles.

Immediate Positioning

Route finding at this level calls upon such primitive skills as the ability to distinguish between sheep tracks and footpaths; to recognise the shiny marks on rock which betray the passage of walkers; and to trace out a feasible line over and among boulders and pinnacles of rock.

Bring each of these skills together, add a dash of intuition, and you have the route finding insight of a seasoned hill walker.

Mountain Features *(Fig 29)*

When route finding it can help to think of mountains as being shaped from two distinct feature systems: protruding ones (slopes, shoulders, ridges and summits) and indented ones (cols, stream beds, corries and valleys). In each system one feature tends to lead on to the next, giving connected and logical lines of ascent or descent. Not that things always turn out as smoothly as we might wish. A ridge, for instance, might suddenly rear up as a knife-edged arête, or a stream might funnel down a steep-sided gully. In these cases transferring from ridge to corrie, or stream bed to shoulder (in other words from one feature system to the next) can create more problems than it solves. Sometimes the only solution is to retrace the route back to more gentle terrain.

In identifying those mountain features most liable to sudden change of character, perhaps we can apply ourselves to a route finding challenge with fractionally more chance of success than a rat in a maze! The following are suggestions of how to do this.

Stream Beds

Streams have a habit of diving over cliffs during their tumbling descent of the mountain – an unhappy conclusion to the day should we be following one at the time. Up or down, they rarely offer more than a temporary solution to a route finding problem.

Corries *(hanging valleys, cwms, cirques)*

Though guarded by steep entries, access to these major glaciated features is rarely difficult. The problem comes later when trying to find a feasible exit up their characteristically craggy headwalls.

Cols *(notches, gaps)*

In taking huge bites out of ridge crests, these features become the natural crossroads of the mountains. It may be practical to ascend to a col from a corrie, but then perhaps not to exit from the col on to the crest of the ridge itself. Broad Stand above the col of Mickledore on Scafell is a classic example.

Sometimes the converse is true; at each side of the col a loose gully will descend at an alarming angle. In this case what might have been earmarked as emergency escapes from the ridge are now shown to be traps. The gullies descending from Glencoe's Aonach Eagach Ridge are well known for this deception.

Shoulders *(spurs, broad ridges)*

Glaciers truncated many such features where they protruded into the corrie or valley floor. As a result lines of cliffs now guard their bases. It would be very unusual not to find a way through by outflanking the worst of them on one side or the other before striking upwards towards the crest.

Ridges

These pronounced features, highways of the hills, appeared during glaciation as slender remnants from the scouring of neighbouring corries. This explains why a ridge may begin in the valley as a series of broad and gentle humps, narrowing as it rises (Helvellyn's Striding Edge springs to mind) to a toothed crest with precipitous sides – exhilarating in good weather, terrifying in bad.

Fig 29   Typical mountain features. This mountainside in North Wales (the northern slopes of the Glyders) contains a typical rugged mix of ridges, rocky cirques and cliffs. Note how the walking routes (dotted lines) avoid the difficult places and ascend over broad ridges and shoulders or intervening valleys, while the scrambling routes (dashed lines) seek out narrow ridges and major fault lines on the cliffs. The smoother sections of rock are ascended by rock climbers using ropes and other protection equipment. An important skill is being able to recognise these various types of route from the map.

41

Terrain

If we can put geography to one side for a moment, we might classify all the different kinds of terrain encountered while hill walking under one of three headings: hard (rock), soft (vegetation) and fluid (water).

Rock

Bare rock is mostly confined to eroded footpaths, narrow ridge crests, and unstable accumulations of small stones found below cliffs (scree slopes). The cliffs themselves and the fields of large boulders far below them are the more obvious examples of intractable terrain.

Rocky paths and ridge crests add variety and interest to a walk, but can be tiring on the feet and nerves. Scree slopes are less precarious than appearances suggest, but nevertheless make tiring and unpleasant lines of ascent. Scree offers an opportunity for rapid descent, albeit at some risk to boots and backsides. If the slope also contains rock outcrops there is an added danger (apart from the obvious one of falling over them) of cascading stones on to people below.

Conventional paths will try to avoid cliff faces altogether, although some scenically interesting routes are able to find a way through without getting too involved in rock scrambling (the Devil's Kitchen path out of Cwm Idwal is a fine example). That said, the chances of successfully pioneering a new walking route up or down a major cliff barrier are quite remote.

Boulder fields may be counted among the more frustrating types of hill terrain we have the misfortune to encounter from time to time. It is difficult enough maintaining direction through these mantraps, let alone rhythm. If the boulders are covered with moss or lichen the problems are multiplied. Boulder fields are usually found lurking lower down the hillside than scree slopes, often in a level basin well below the cliff face which spawned them.

Vegetation

Vegetation is also scaled in several magnitudes. If you can walk over it (grass) or between it (trees) there is usually little to worry about. It is the intermediate, ankle-grabbing type which makes life difficult:

Dense scrub presents a thorny problem in young forestry plantations or in wooded valleys, whereas clumpy heather is more likely to interfere with walking at higher levels. In this case pieces of exposed rock found on ridge crests might give some temporary respite. A combination of heather and boulders littering the valley floor is the most insidious of all. Bracken proliferates on some lower slopes from summer through to late autumn; an ugly plant, inhabited by exotic insects and bewildered sheep.

Sheep-grazed turf offers the most pleasant walking terrain, although it is rather less accommodating when steeply inclined. The slightest dew or ground frost renders such slopes untenable to bipeds, whereas the sheep – more firmly anchored – move about them untroubled.

Water

Mountains receive much higher levels of rainfall than neighbouring lowlands, and it certainly shows!

Small mountain streams present few difficulties except when attempting to cross during torrential rain. Even then the force behind foaming water is sometimes less than appearances might suggest. A greater danger lurks when attempting to cross rivers in spate lower down the hillside. This can be a severe problem in remote areas of Scotland where there may be no easy alternative route of descent (*see* Chapter 6).

Marshland may be identified at a distance, betrayed by the tell-tale colour of the vegetation it supports. The distinction will be less obvious in poorly drained areas, such as the Peak District, or during very wet summers. Even the most established of paths may be forced to submerge for a boggy interlude while crossing a shallow col or when circling a lake-filled basin. Faced with that kind of difficulty our best ally will be a good pair of boots – or a stoical attitude towards wet feet.

5 Map Reading

No matter how thorough your preparation, or how broad your experience, route finding in the mountains will always be plagued by dozens of little uncertainties. These need not arise because your plan or sense of direction has broken down, merely because you would feel happier with some outside confirmation of your position and your intuitive route finding decisions. More rarely it happens that visibility is so poor or the terrain so featureless that continuous navigation with a map and compass becomes an essential aid to route finding. This more precise aspect of map reading is the topic of Chapter 14.

Consulting the map from time to time (and compass if necessary) avoids compounding small errors into big mistakes. Otherwise the chances are that when the map is eventually consulted, it merely confirms your worst fears – namely that you are indeed lost. Think of it this way: suppose when faced by a fork in the path you intuitively, but mistakenly, turn left. After a few strides you become less certain. A glance at the map now would reveal the error and put you back on course. The mistake has cost you nothing. But if you ignore that seed of doubt and continue (the temptation is always to do so) then your mistake and subsequent embarrassment grow with every stride. If you *know* your position, then you are likely to be on route; if you *think* you know your position, then there is a fair chance you are lost.

CARRYING CONVENIENCE

A map hidden away at the bottom of the rucksack is likely to stay there. Even a zipped lid pocket can not be considered accessible. You will be astonished to discover (in retrospect) your reluctance to interrupt rhythm in order to perform even the simplest of tasks, such as stopping to remove a rucksack. You must make it easy for yourself.

Some people like to carry their map and compass on neck cords; the map being protected by a transparent plastic wallet and folded to reveal the relevant area. This method offers maximum accessibility, though at some cost to patience on windy days or when scrambling. A common alternative is to fold the map as before, but now to carry both it and the compass in an outside jacket pocket (while protecting them from rain with an ordinary plastic bag). This works best in a jacket fitted with a special map pocket, otherwise the rucksack waistbelt obstructs their removal from a conventional pocket at hip level.

Well-used maps soon begin to disintegrate under the repeated strain of folding and unfolding, particularly when damp. To combat this it may be worth covering one or both sides with a transparent self-adhesive film, available from stationers or art shops. The cost of this protection may exceed that of the map itself, so its application is probably worth while only on your most used maps. The Ordnance Survey experiment with waterproof maps from time to time, but consider that the majority of their customers are unwilling to pay the increased cost.

SETTING THE MAP
(Figs 30 to 33)

It is common to feel disorientated when beginning a walk among unfamiliar hills. Our preconceived image of the landscape never quite matches what we see around us, and we are faced with the odd situation of a map seeming to be more real than the land it represents. The cure is to align the map with the terrain. At last this makes sense out of nonsense – as if laying the paper pattern on the cloth – and brings the hills alive. There

are two ways of setting the map: by eye and by compass.

If visibility is good and you are able to recognise a distinctive peak or other major feature, then simply swivel the open map until the line from your position to this target coincides with your actual line of sight. Naturally this assumes you know your location to begin with and are able to identify it on the map, but having left the road only five minutes before this is surely not too much to ask. Once set in this way, the north arrow on the map (and by definition the top of the map) will point north in reality.

If it is misty or if you are unable positively to identify a landmark, then the

Fig 30   Setting the map by compass.

Relating Map Information to the Landscape

Fig 31   Even on a clear day the way forward is not always obvious.

map is set by compass. This is very easy. Simply place the compass on the map so that it is level, and allow the needle to settle. Then gently swivel both map and compass together until the north needle (painted red) points towards the top of the map.

By holding the map in this same set orientation, you now have in your hands a detailed miniature of the landscape that stretches before you. It is this bird's eye view of the hidden terrain ahead that becomes your most powerful ally in prediction.

MEASURING DISTANCE AND ESTIMATING TIME

By itself the concept of distance to be travelled to the next landmark rarely has direct relevance; a prediction instead of the time it will take to travel a given distance will be a more useful indicator. Time estimates have been mentioned already in the context of route planning, but in this context the period will be very much shorter. A quick estimate can be arrived at

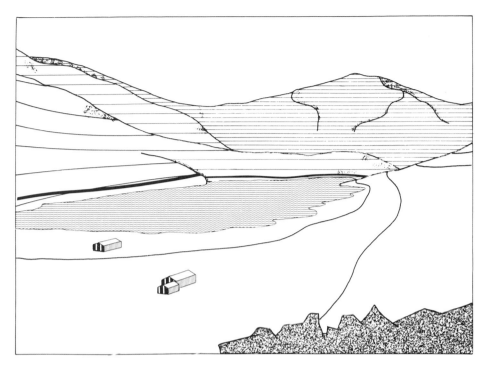

Fig 32   *Maps extract the essential features of a landscape ...*

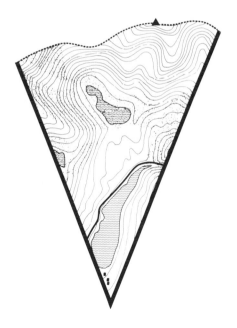

Fig 33   *... and provide the bird's-eye view which enables us to 'see' beyond obtruding ridges (shaded areas).*

by allowing twelve minutes for each kilometre travelled on the map (recalling that this is equivalent to the side of a grid square), plus one minute for each contour line crossed on the way (assuming these are at ten-metre intervals). This formula is none other than a scaled-down version of Naismith's Rule, which was described as an aid to route planning in Chapter 3.

Visibility is sometimes so poor that the only safe way to locate your next turning point is to calculate its distance from your present position and then to pace it out according to a precalibrated formula. This technique, discussed more fully in Chapter 14, is especially valuable when route finding over featureless terrain or if drifting snow has obscured the path.

Confirming Position

Sometimes we need reassurance that we are where we think we are. As hinted earlier, these can prove to be two very different places.

First, locate on the map your presumed position. Then, using the compass as described above, set the map to the terrain. Hopefully, you will now be able to predict the location of landmarks around you (such as by saying 'there is a lake in a valley to my left' and so on). If the first three or four predictions prove correct then you can relax. If not – and it is no use pretending some boggy hollow is the lake you wished it to be – then it is wisest to swallow your pride and admit to being lost. If visibility is good there is no need to despair; a similar but more elaborate procedure (using the compass) can be used to determine your real position. This is described in Chapter 14. If visibility is poor, however, for the time being you can consider yourself in trouble. What you should have done, although it is too late now for recrimination, was continuously to monitor progress by identifying on the map the succession of small-scale features as they were encountered.

INTERPRETATION *(Fig 34)*

The degree of detail shown on a map depends very much on its scale. For instance a 1:25,000 map will differentiate between slopes of scree and slopes of boulders, whereas a 1:50,000 map simply will not have the space. Often it is enough merely to distinguish between major mountain features – ridges and valleys, cliffs and scree, slopes and plateaux, peaks and cols, and so on – for which purpose either scale is adequate.

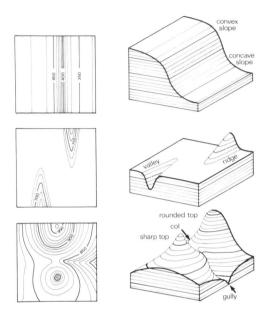

Fig 34   Interpretation of contour lines.

Much of the information about slope and shape is communicated with the help of contour lines (introduced in a general way with regard to route planning in Chapter 3). While not practical to set down here all the subtle groupings of contour lines (they are as many and as varied as the features they represent) the few examples shown in *Fig 34* will indicate the potential. One general point to bear in mind is that contours are unable to describe features which fall entirely within two successive lines. A sharp dip in a ridge, for instance, or even a substantial grass knoll may not be recorded on the map at all.

Contour lines also reveal the average gradient of a slope. To make this calculation you need three pieces of information: the height interval between contour lines (this is usually ten metres, but you will need to check on the map itself); the horizontal distance between top and bottom of the slope (measured on the map and translated to metres using the scale); and the number of contour lines crossed during the ascent (it may be easier to count every fifth line – which is shown in emphasised colour – and then to multiply by fifty). For example, 5 lines (or one emphasised line) crossed in a distance of 100m (50m in 100m) indicates a gradient of 1 in 2 (1:2) an angle at which you might expect to adopt a zigzag line of ascent. Gradients may also be expressed as a percentage (50 per cent in this example). As an aid to visualisation a useful exercise is to assign these numbers to the sides of an imaginary (or sketched) right-angled tri-angle, in which the hypotenuse represents the slope to be ascended. Each gradient has its own connotation, although a sinister grouping of the contour lines is sufficient indication in itself that trouble lies ahead. Note, however, that for reasons of space intermediate lines are sometimes faded out on steeper slopes in favour of retaining the emphasised lines at 50m intervals.

Having fixed in your mind the shape and steepness of the terrain you are about to encounter, the conventional terrain symbols – scree, marsh, and so on – ought to confirm, or at least not contradict, what you see around you.

Contour lines are unable to depict the very steepest slopes because they would then be so bunched together as to appear as one. Cliff symbols are employed instead. It ought to be possible to discern from their orientation the difference between cliff top and cliff bottom – an important distinction as you will agree. Unfortunately some maps designate outcrops with what appears to be a reversed cliff symbol. Usually the ambiguity can be resolved simply by studying neighbouring contour lines to get some feeling for the general trend of the slope.

6 The Unexpected

Sometimes things don't quite turn out as expected: repulsed by impenetrable cliffs; forced into lengthy diversions; battered by sudden squalls of hail and storm force winds – at times it seems as if a conspiracy is being worked against us. Darkness delivers the final blow, overtaking us when we are tired and demoralised and still so very high on the mountain. Maybe it should never happen, but it does. The spectre of the unexpected haunts us all.

OBSTACLES

For each obstacle identified there lurks another undreamed of, but here are a few anyway.

Walls, Fences and Forestry

Such is the enormity of the surveyor's task that information on current maps is sometimes twenty years out of date. Within that period it is likely that new fences will have been erected, bridges washed away, and paths re-routed. In five years a plantation of young fir trees becomes a spiny jungle.

Common sense and consideration tells us not to climb walls or fences, but the occasion will arise when no reasonable alternative presents itself. In that case it is only fair to spend a few minutes looking for the sturdiest post or firmest stone to support an unauthorised crossing. As for the forest of firs, it is they that will be inflicting the damage. With luck you'll find a stream bed cutting through to open ground beyond –

wet feet being a lesser evil than gouged eyes and a painful stoop.

Crags and Gullies

Maps rarely distinguish between the benign and the malicious in crags and gullies. If progress is halted by unexpectedly difficult terrain, suspect a route finding error before blaming lack of conviction on your part. The golden rule when confronting natural barriers such as these is never to climb up what you cannot climb down (and vice versa during descent). Most of us have an embarrassing tale to tell about the day we ignored that advice.

Rivers in Spate *(Figs 35 & 36)*

Water drains fast and furiously from the mountains in stormy weather, and to be confronted by a raging torrent which six hours previously had been a trickling stream is a shocking finale to a long and tiring day.

If the experience promises merely to be unpleasant, with no risk of being swept away, then once having found the optimum crossing – probably a broad and shallow stretch with low banks free of partly submerged bushes – it remains only to remove socks (but retain boots and gaiters), roll up clothing, and get on with it, facing upstream and shuffling sideways while using a stick or ice-axe for added support. Though certain to emerge dripping wet and stunned by cold, this is surely better than the complete dousing risked by leaping between spaced and treacherous boulders. As a

Fig 35   *In just a few hours this trickling stream . . .*

Fig 36   *. . . became a foaming torrent, and subsided almost as quickly.*

final precaution it would be wise to unclip the rucksack waistbelt, so that at least if you do slip you will not be stranded like a tortoise on its back.

Rivers look ugly and powerful at dangerous crossings, and you will need little persuasion to seek every possible alternative. This might involve a detour far upstream to ford instead a series of smaller tributaries. Another option is to wait for the water to subside, normally a matter of a few hours but possibly involving a bivouac. Otherwise a serious river crossing will demand elaborate rope protection, familiarity with the techniques and a fair measure of desperation.

Collapsing snow banks are an added haz-ard in the winter season. The biggest worry here is being carried away by the stream – even a narrow one – to become trapped where it disappears beneath a snow bridge.

Deep snow may conceal streams and small lakes altogether. In the gloom of dusk an unsuspecting walker might fail to notice the tell-tale signs, so that by the time its treacherous surface crumbles beneath his feet he is already some distance from the bank. Numbing cold, a heavy rucksack and cumbersome footwear seal his fate. Sadly the incidence of such accidents is not rare. Careful study of the map is insufficient safeguard in itself because not all small lakes and streams are marked. The imaginative and vigilant stand the best chance.

51

WEATHER

Such is the fickle nature of British weather that we have grown to expect the unexpected. Consequently spare clothing and waterproof suits are packed as a standard precaution at any time of year. But for all that, sudden winds and electric storms may still catch us unawares.

Wind

Battling against an unexpected headwind causes delay, weariness and cold. In these conditions it may be wise to seek a longer but less exposed alternative. Sometimes this means simply reversing the planned route so that the headwind is met during the outward leg.

Violent and unpredictable gusts of wind make ridge traversing an uncertain business, but provided the ridge is not steep sided you may be able to complete the crossing in the relative calm a few metres below the crest.

In winter the smooth snow surfaces of domed mountains, such as those typical of the Cairngorms and Carneddau, present little resistance to the winds which sweep across their summit plateaux. Gusts of over 200 k.p.h. have been recorded. Even in winds of half that strength the pressure exerted on a body clad in bulky winter clothing and carrying a rucksack is tremendous. Normal upright progress can prove impossible, and you may find yourself reduced to a crab-crawl while using your ice-axe to prevent being blown across the ice.

Lightning

It may seem remarkable for anyone to speak

Fig 37   An electric storm over Tryfan, North Wales.

of lightning danger from personal experience, but the fact remains that a fair proportion of hill walkers will at some time suffer the minor effects of electrical discharge. Usually confined to tingling sensations and blue flashes around the body, a closer strike may induce involuntary muscle convulsions. A close or direct strike, an extremely rare occurrence, may prove fatal.

In deference to the invincible nature of lightning, all precautions taken against it can only be defensive. The first is to make yourself as inconspicuous as possible. Summits and ridge crests are clearly places to avoid, but – less obviously – so too are cracks in cliff faces and gaps beneath boulders. This is because electricity likes to travel down damp cracks and prefers to short through our watery bodies than jump a dry air gap. Statistics and physical theory advise us to sit out lightning storms on open slopes of broken boulders. Apparently the correct posture is sitting on a rucksack with hands on knees (while no doubt the best mental attitude is one of stoical good humour). If it is any consolation, violent storms rarely last more than an hour or two.

There is no evidence to suggest that hardware such as ice-axe and crampons increase the likelihood of a nearby strike; besides, you may later regret having thrown them over a cliff in panic. That said, it would take a well-disciplined mind to resist moving them to a respectful distance for the duration of the storm. Superstition it may be, but it can't do any harm.

GROUND CONDITIONS

Rubber boot soles grip extremely well on most surfaces. Unfortunately wet grass, greasy rock and all varieties of snow and ice are not among them.

Grass

When angled at forty degrees and coated with frost or light rain, sheep-grazed turf offers about as much traction as a greasy pole. Given the luxury of choice, ascent – as opposed to descent or traversing – offers the most reliable escape (fear injects a powerful strength into fingernails).

Rocks

Clean rock provides adequate friction even when wet; it is the coating of moss and lichen which makes boulders so slippery. Some rocky paths and scrambles are little affected by damp, whereas others – for no apparent reason – become twice as difficult. Constant scuffing removes moss and lichen from popular paths and scrambles, so these routes are the least affected. If necessary, you can improve friction by removing your stockings and pulling them on again over the outsides of your boots. It really works!

The stocking technique also works to some degree on *verglas* – water vapour which has condensed on cold rock and then frozen into a thin, transparent layer. However, if at all possible it would be wiser to retreat from the encounter. Frozen rain (rainfall which has frozen in its contact with cold rock) is even more lethal than verglas because the greater accumulation of ice obscures edges and cracks which otherwise might have provided some meagre means of support.

Loose Rock

Despite all precautions you may occasionally dislodge rocks while moving on steep terrain. Even a small stone can inflict serious injury by the time it has gathered speed, so you owe somebody a warning. A shouted *'below'* is the accepted term, and make it loud – this is no time for self-conscious restraint.

Snow and Ice

Snow and ice accumulate over periods varying from hours to months, although the circumstances under which they do so are generally predictable (*see* Chapter 9).

Genuinely unpredictable patches of snow – perhaps encountered late in the season during the descent of a north facing slope – are often the remnants of cornices, deep gully drifts or avalanche debris. They are usually confined to a small area and are therefore avoidable.

ILLNESS AND INJURY

Minor injuries such as blisters, muscle strain, cramp, twisted ankles, sunburn, mild snow-blindness, and the early stages of frost-bite are more likely to be sustained as a result of carelessness than genuine misfortune. We all make mistakes, though, and the section on basic first aid in Chapter 15 lists some remedies.

Major injury or hypothermia (exposure) are more likely to be the culminating disaster of a series of errors than the consequence of an isolated mistake. However, even if you consider yourself immune you might be called upon to help someone from another party. With expert help probably hours away, action taken in the interim may literally make the difference between life and death. Chapter 15 indicates some of what can be done.

BENIGHTMENT

Unexpected delay can often be traced back to miscalculations at the route planning stage, or to failure to modify the plan in the face of deteriorating conditions; whereas at other times the culprit is pure misadventure. In either case, ordinary delay soon extends into benightment.

In high summer, assuming you have adequate spare clothing, the prospect of benightment in the British mountains is not a worrying one. Temperatures rarely fall to dangerously low levels, and provided you can escape the wind and rain the few hours of darkness – however interminable they may seem at the time – will leave you little the worse for the experience.

The decision to bivouac depends very much on the combination of circumstances; for instance whether or not you are lost at the time, or on the viability of continuing the descent by moonlight or the aid of a headtorch. Alternatively it could be forced by medical implications, such as if someone in the party is showing the early signs of hypothermia. Chapter 15 deals with this special dilemma in more detail.

If you do decide to bivouac, the half-hour or so spent looking for shelter – perhaps behind a mountain wall or underneath a boulder – will more than repay the effort. A survival bag wins valuable extra protection against wind and damp ground, despite the fact that it will eventually become wet inside from condensation. The principles of maintaining warmth are concerned with minimising the surface area of your body (but without restricting blood flow by curling up too tightly), and with applying extra insulation to the head and to those parts of the body in contact with the ground. Huddling together helps, and if two people can get into a single survival bag then so much the better.

A bivouac in the period late autumn to late spring would be very much more serious, particularly if it had been forced by poor ground conditions and hostile weather. Although a survival bag and extra clothing are considered essential emergency equipment at this time of year, the protection they offer will not be enough to secure a comfortable night. 'Survival' is the key word when planning for emergencies; but often it is not enough simply to survive the

Fig 38   Late autumn evening on the summit of Glyder Fach: difficult ground conditions, approaching bad weather and failing light.

night – an outcome which is unlikely to be in doubt – but to emerge at daybreak in a fit state to continue the descent, possibly in deteriorating conditions. In fact, it would almost always have been better to persevere with the descent through the hours of darkness.

Planned bivouacs are, of course, a very different proposition. When comfortable and secure, the sense of isolation instead of being frightening now serves to enrich the experience.

PRESERVING THE UNEXPECTED

Up until this point these tales of the unexpected have evoked nothing but misery and hardship and danger, which we would do anything in our power to escape. There is though, one element of the unexpected we must preserve at all costs – that of spontaneous variation. Without it the prospect of doggedly adhering to route plans has about it that musty air of predictability we have come to the mountains to escape. Some of the best days grow from a capricious decision to explore beyond the limits of the plan. The urge to exceed expectations is in us all.

ROCK
SCRAMBLING

Fig 39   Exhilarating scramble on Pen Yr Ole Wen.

7 Rock Scrambling

When does a walk become a scramble? Most hill walks involve a short scramble – if only to reach a summit block perched above a cone of boulders – so perhaps the distinction is academic. Some sort of definition might be cobbled together from the notion that scrambling implies the use of handholds. But one person may cling nervously to a narrow ridge, along which another will stroll calmly upright. With the fate of those two people in mind, perhaps the definition should emphasise the different consequences of a fall. More often than not a fall while walking would give us no more than a bloody nose and a temporary limp, whereas a fall while scrambling would be horrific. That, however, takes no account of the hazards that face walker and scrambler alike. The truth is that any attempt at demarcation between walking and scrambling will be arbitrary – as indeed it is between scrambling and rock climbing.

If there must be a definition at all, it will derive from different attitudes held towards danger: walkers avoid it; rock climbers live with it; scramblers flirt with it. If scrambling is at all dangerous, why do it? In a sense scrambling puts back into hill walking what paths and cairns have taken out; it puts back uncertainty. At its best, scrambling whips up a feeling of intoxicated exhilaration; at worst, a creeping fear. Mostly it invites sensations somewhere between the two.

In choosing to go scrambling we fabricate challenges by deliberately exposing ourselves to difficulty, danger and uncertainty. We do that by committing ourselves to one of the mountain's more intractable features – it may be a ridge, a rocky shoulder or a gully. Sometimes the ascent unfolds without incident, at other times with a struggle, and occasionally not at all. We go up there armed with cunning, agility and mischievous determination. But we know when and how to escape because we have common sense in our heads, a rope in our rucksacks, and we are not afraid to use either.

WHERE TO GO

Each of the three high mountain regions of Britain – Scotland, the Lake District and North Wales – offer plenty of opportunities for the scrambler. Hills in other regions are generally too small or too gentle to provide anything of more than a diversionary nature. Ireland too, though not detailed in this book, has good scrambling within its more rugged mountain regions, in particular Macgillicuddy's Reeks of the far south-west.

Walking guides describe a few of the easier scrambles (though often affecting mock terror), while the climbing guides will briefly (and disparagingly) mention some of the harder ones. More recently, guidebooks have been written specifically about scrambles. Their approach is to indicate the character and whereabouts of worthwhile routes, but without going into too much detail about where to put your hands and feet (and so preserve the sense of adventure). A summary of these guides will be found in the bibliography.

Scotland

Some of the best and certainly most documented routes will be found in the west coast regions of Skye, Ben Nevis and Glencoe. Some famous outings are frequently referred to as scrambles when in fact they include sections of rock climbing (the Tower Ridge on Ben Nevis, the Cuillin Ridge of Skye). Nevertheless, there is no shortage of genuine scrambles of the highest quality, for example, the Aonach Eagach Ridge above Glencoe.

Intrinsically there is little difference between scrambling in Scotland and in any other mountainous region. What differences there are generally relate to scale and climate: in seeking out the steeper flanks of high mountains you will often find yourself on sunless north faces where – unlike in North Wales or the Lake District – spring snow often endures until June.

Lake District

The Lake District boasts a long association with scrambling. To this day its fell walkers seem that much more willing to get their hands out of their pockets. In addition to notorious obstacles (Broad Stand on Scafell) and some delightful miniature climbs (Pillar Rock), there are worthwhile ascents at all levels of difficulty. These include uncomplicated ridges (Striding Edge on Helvellyn) and insecure gullies (Lord's Rake on Scafell).

A dynamic climate and suitable geology have endowed the Lake District with another type of scramble – the gill climb. The techniques required are closer to open-air pot-holing than mountaineering, but the adventures are no less rewarding.

Fig 40   Broad Stand, Scafell: a short but notorious impasse.

Fig 41   Dungeon Ghyll, Langdale.

North Wales

The potential in North Wales equals that of the Lake District, although the evidence is not so obvious. Popular ridges (Crib Goch on Snowdon, Bristly Ridge on Glyder Fach) are always crowded during fine weekends, whereas the more difficult and elusive scrambles (Dolmen Ridge on Glyder Fach, Clogwyn y Person Arete) are ascended much less often. Intriguing routes ascend remote buttresses in regions neglected by climbers and walkers alike. Here the thrill of exploration more than compensates for any lack of reputation.

PERSONAL EQUIPMENT

Clothing

There is no reason why clothing used for hill walking should not be equally suitable for scrambling (*see* Chapter 2). Choose wisely in the first instance and there will be no duplication. Nevertheless, there are slight shifts in priority when buying equipment specifically with scrambling in mind. These are outlined below.

Footwear

Top quality summer boots are ideal for scrambling because they are light and neat. Avoid cheap versions fitted with PVC soles (poor friction) and those constructed from very flexible soles and soft uppers. You will be looking for a boot which is firm but not cumbersome. Trainers and other ultralight footwear are not suitable. While giving good grip on dry rock, they offer conspicuously poor support on vegetation and greasy boulders.

Legwear

Here you will be looking for something neat but which will stretch to accommodate high leg movements. Breeches and tracksuit trousers are both suitable.

Midwear

Comments applied to midwear in Chapter 2 are no less relevant here, except that free shoulder movement now assumes the highest priority.

Outerwear

A windproof overshirt or simple anorak is neater and cheaper than a heavy jacket covered in pockets (rock damage is inevitable). For the same reasons a basic waterproof jacket may be more practical than an expensive model in Gore-Tex or similar material. Hip-length designs are less restrictive than those cut to three-quarter length. Note that waterproof overtrousers severely impede leg movement and are worth carrying only for the approach and descent.

Gloves

Mitts and full gloves lack sensitivity on anything more technical than the easiest scrambles, so for cold or wet weather a pair of fingerless gloves is well worth having. Gloves are also essential for rope handling, for which full gloves are better, but the fingerless type will do. There is little point buying an expensive pair because they soon become lost or threadbare. Wool gives better friction than nylon on wet rock, although it does wear more rapidly.

Fig 42   Traversing Crib Goch on the famous Snowdon Horseshoe.

Rucksacks

An ordinary daysack will have more than enough capacity. Simple, frameless models are less unwieldy than those fitted with elaborate harnesses, although a narrow waistbelt will help to stabilise the load. Ultra-lightweight models in ripstop nylon cannot withstand much rock abrasion.

ON THE MOUNTAIN

Movement and Style *(Fig 43)*

Scrambling comes naturally. The physical and mental procedure of moving from one ledge to the next will present few serious difficulties to anyone reasonably agile and unperturbed by impressive surroundings. Having said that, there are many advantages in developing a good scrambling style which conserves energy, endows confidence and prepares you for the really tough obstacles. The key word here is *developing*. Good style emerges gradually and without anguish. If you try to learn it as you would a dance step your rhythm and balance will crumble.

Being very much a personal thing, style has little to do with outward appearances of movement such as 'grace' or 'athleticism'. Nevertheless, there are two main basic principles common to all good styles. There

Fig 43   An effective scrambling style. Note the low hand position and upright stance. This style is less tiring and more secure than 'hugging' the rock or making long reaches, and allows you to see the next set of footholds.

*Fig 44   This ridge gains Snowdon Summit by interesting
scrambling and avoids the patches of spring snow
on the normal route (far right). Route finding on
ridges ought to be obvious, but one can unintentionally
stray on to the more difficult flanks.*

are sound mechanical reasons why it is best to maintain a reasonably upright attitude (as opposed to hugging the rock) and why it is best to resist the temptation always to reach for uncomfortably high hand and footholds. But your *interpretation* of these basic principles is more about doing what works than about doing what looks right.

This undisciplined learning process of style and technique accounts for a lot of the interest in scrambling – delve too deeply and it becomes a chore. We have said enough already.

Route Finding

Much of what was said under the previous heading applies equally well here; the skill of route finding over steep terrain is acquired largely by trial and error. However, as with route finding over more gentle terrain, a couple of ugly situations repeat themselves with unsettling frequency – and the sooner you get to know about them the better.

63

*Fig 45   These two gullies on Tryfan ascend its East Face with
relative ease. Route finding in gullies is usually simple,
but note the subsidiary gully start used by the right-hand
route to avoid the sinister and difficult lower sections
of the main gully (identified as dark fissures).*

The Irreversible Move

Rock climbers know all about this demon,
which they confront on almost every route.
Climb or scramble, that move marks the
threshold of temptation – cross it and there
is no going back. A typical irreversible
move is one to overcome a little blank wall
topped by a thatch of tufted grass. Imagine
wishing to descend having had second
thoughts, clinging to a crumbling sod, while
trying to locate the solitary tiny foothold
which helped you on the way up!

The Mantrap

This is really the converse of the first ugly
situation. The trap is more commonly
entered during descent, although it can be a
feature of a ridge crest. Suppose that in
order to further your descent you slide
down a holdless rock slab to land on a
comfortingly large ledge. Now take stock
of the situation: vertical and unclimbable
rock falls to left and right; the holdless (and
equally unclimbable) slab rises above; while
below – what is below? Peering over the

*Fig 46   This complex face route on Scafell (Lord's Rake and West
Wall Traverse) uses a lucky combination of terraces,
rakes and gullies to gain the summit. Route finding
on such routes is frequently far from obvious.*

edge to find out you discover another
holdless slab, except that this one is twenty
metres long and ends in space. Sheep
regularly make this mistake. Sometimes,
through the mist, you can hear one bleating
plaintively from high up on the crags. Or is
it a scrambler?

Special Hazards

Loose rock and unreliable greenery account
for much of the nervous energy expended
during scrambling, while unexpected bad
weather and poor ground conditions con-

tribute to the general anxiety.

Loose rock is more of a problem than it
ever was while walking, not least because
now when you dispatch a rock down the
hillside there is every chance you will soon
follow. A rotten spike – like a rotten tooth –
will usually give up its treacherous secret to
a sharp jab from the fist. Don't *trust* it, *test* it.

The one exception to the 'test it' rule is
when a partially jammed boulder blocks
your exit from a narrow gully. If the
scramble is a popular one then the chances
are in your favour: if the boulder meant to
go at all, you surmise, it would have gone

65

already. On a less frequented route you will have no such reassurance.

Perverse scrambles ascend rock which is rotten to the core: nothing is safe. The best you can do here is distribute your weight evenly through all the limbs at your disposal (you can never have too many) and hope that if one point of attachment fails the others will hold. On this sort of ground there is some considerable danger of loosing rocks on to your partner below. A climbing helmet would deflect the smaller ones (and give valuable protection in a fall) but their use for scrambling is not yet widespread.

Rock is not the only thing you grab hold of when scrambling. Grass, heather, saplings – nothing is sacred when you are short of a handhold. Each plant responds differently to your touch: some snap off straight away; others tease with a slow ripping noise; while yet more wait until your full weight is suspended and then depart unannounced. Scrambling is truly an uncertain business.

8 Rope Protected Scrambles

Roped scrambling resembles early rock climbing both in its objectives and in the methods employed to achieve them. In that sense it has barely changed in a hundred years. Today's ropes are very much stronger and the techniques a little more refined, but the central principle of safety-lining (as opposed to rope-swarming) remains intact. In scrambling the rope plays an entirely passive role until called upon – if ever – to arrest a fall or facilitate retreat: no more, no less.

Roped scrambles differ from rock climbs in that not all the ascent is protected. The rope may be used only once or twice in three hundred metres, perhaps to safeguard an especially difficult step in a gully or exposed part of a ridge. On many scrambles the rope remains in the rucksack throughout.

Deciding when to use the rope is never easy, and some people feel confident scrambling unroped where others never could. There are so many variables that it is impossible to lay down firm guidelines. What follows is therefore a simple exposition of equipment and procedures. The decision of when and where to apply them must be entirely your own.

PROCEDURES

Tying On *(Figs 47 & 48)*

If you can, stop to tie on at a reasonably spacious ledge, otherwise someone will trip over a rucksack and launch into premature

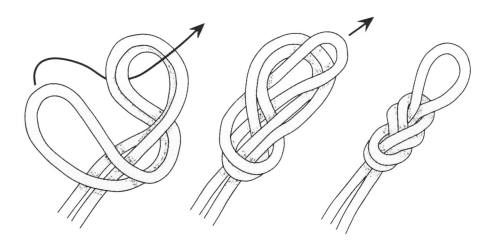

Fig 47   Knots for tying on and anchoring. Figure-of-eight – note the distinctive final form.

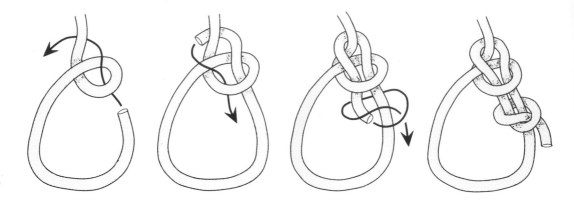

Fig 48   *Bowline – some people learn this knot aided by the mnemonic 'the rabbit comes out of its hole, around the tree and back down the hole'. Note the spare end finally secured by a stopper knot.*

flight. To uncoil the rope, resist the temptation to lay it down on the ledge in a neat coil – it will surely tangle. Believe it or not, the way to avoid tangles is to remove loops from the coil individually and cast them down to form a loose pile. Take special care at this time to avoid standing on the rope (*see* 'Rope Care', page 73).

When using a single rope the leader and second will tie on to opposite ends using a bowline knot tied snugly around the waist, while a third person will tie on at the middle using a figure-of-eight knot. If the group is larger than three then the leader and second will tie on and proceed as normal to the top of the steep section, afterwards throwing down the rope end for each extra member to tie on and follow in turn.

When using a doubled rope the leader ties on at the middle (using the figure-of-eight), while the second ties to the two ends using bowlines.

Finding an Anchor *(Figs 49 to 51)*

Having tied on, the next job is to locate a suitable anchor point on which to secure the second. This might be a rock spike, a tree or a jammed stone. The attachment is made by forming a loop in the main rope and placing it over or around the anchor point. This prevents the second from being pulled off the ledge if the leader falls.

Obviously the anchor point needs to be firm, but that in itself is not enough. What you must do is try to visualise what would happen during a fall, and then consider whether or not the mechanics of your anchor system make sense. Bear in mind that the fall force will transfer to the second along the line of the rope; the pull could come from an unexpected angle – upwards, sideways or diagonally. If there is any doubt whatsoever about the security of the main anchor point, standard practice is to arrange a back-up anchor point.

The securing loop for the anchor is

*Fig 49   An anchor securing loop is formed by a figure-of-eight knot
tied with a large end loop. The anchor securing loop (which is
taut), belayer and rope to second are all in line so the belayer
cannot be pulled sideways if the second falls. Note also the
sitting position to prevent the loop lifting off the anchor point.*

formed using a figure-of-eight knot. If the anchor point needs to be threaded (jammed stone, tree, etc.) the usual practice is to girdle it with a loop of rope and tie the figure-of-eight around the main rope at the waist. If tape slings are carried one of these may be placed over or around the anchor point instead. In this case the figure-of-eight knot is clipped into a locking karabiner, which in turn is clipped into the sling and locked.

When satisfied with the anchor system, and having taken up position for paying-out (belaying) the leader's rope, the second adjusts the knots so that there is no slack in the securing loop. If unable to find a stable position when standing, it is better to sit down. This also limits the risk of the securing loop lifting off the anchor point.

It is not always possible to arrive at an ideal anchor set-up, but with ingenuity and patience something can always be arranged – perhaps by jamming a stone in a crack, or by untying and feeding the rope end through a small hole in the rock. Keep looking, even if it means spending fifteen

69

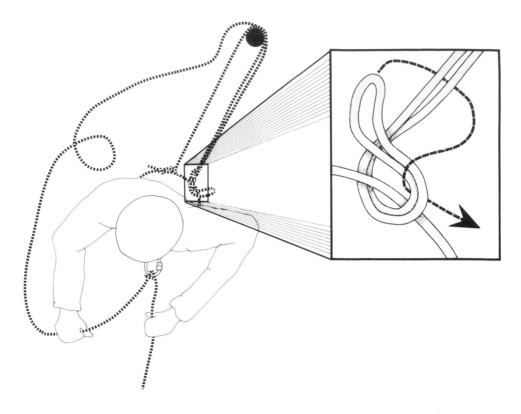

Fig 50   *This shows an alternative anchor securing loop. A loop of rope is drawn around the anchor point and tied-off at the waist using a figure-of-eight knot which incorporates the waist-tie rope.*

minutes or more locating that elusive but all-important anchor point.

Belaying

When firmly anchored, it is the second's job to belay the rope while the leader climbs to a ledge above the obstacle. Clearly this affords minimal security to the leader, who dares not risk a fall. If the leader does slip the second clutches the rope in a prescribed way (described below) and attempts to arrest the fall, although it is unlikely that he will be able to do so before the leader hits

the ground. The force is enormous, more than enough to pull the unwary second off balance. If that happens, and the second loses grip, then the leader will continue to fall the full length of the rope and be severely injured or worse.

Obviously, it would be better if the leader did not fall in the first place. Towards this end it is usual for the most experienced member of the party to take the lead position. Nevertheless, much of the point of this exercise is to prepare for every eventuality, however unlikely and horrifying it may seem.

Fig 51 In this example a tape sling has been looped over the anchor point and the securing loop clipped to it with a locking karabiner.

Choosing a Rope

The choice of rope is very important indeed. Obviously it must be strong, but that in itself is not enough; it must also have dynamic property. This is because you want a fall to be arrested relatively gradually, not jerked to a sudden back-breaking halt. Some ropes – polypropylene and the so-called abseil ropes and hill walkers' confidence ropes among them – stretch very little under load. These are unsuitable for scrambling. Only nylon climbing ropes will have the properties you need.

Climbing ropes are made in diameters ranging from about 8.5mm to 11.5mm, and in lengths from 36m to 50m. A popular choice for rock climbing is 45m of 11mm, but this is much too heavy for taking on a scramble. A good compromise is 36m of 9mm. This will be used double for climbing, allowing you to protect tricky sections of about 15m height (after allowing for the waist knots). It also has sufficient thickness to allow a firm grip in the belayer's hands. A single 11mm rope of 18m length might appear to be a lighter and more manageable alternative, but this would leave insufficient length for abseiling.

Regardless of which make of rope you buy, make sure that it carries the UIAA label of approval.

Forces accumulate rapidly during a fall, so very precise methods of belaying the rope have been developed. Two methods are relevant. The first, which requires no special equipment, applies a braking force using the friction created between the rope and the belayer's back, hips, arms and hands (hence the need for gloves and long-sleeved clothing). The procedure is easier to demonstrate than explain, so it would be a good idea to practise the technique while referring to *Fig 57*.

The second and more foolproof method generates braking friction within a special sliding knot called the *Italian friction hitch*. This is tied around a locking karabiner at the second's waist. *Fig 52* demonstrates how to arrange and operate this system.

When paying out the rope it is wise to maintain a metre or so of slack. This allows the leader to make a sudden move without having to tug on the rope, and also gives some leeway if a tangle develops.

Having overcome the obstacle, the leader

finds an anchor point and secures in the normal way. Only then will the second release the belayed rope. This concept of overlapped security is central to all good rope protection methods. After pulling up any remaining rope, the leader adopts the belay position. On the signal, the second unties the anchor securing loop and prepares to climb. While the second climbs, the leader takes in slack rope as it accumulates. Provided the rope hangs down in a straight line to the second, this means that a slip will be arrested almost immediately and with little risk of injury.

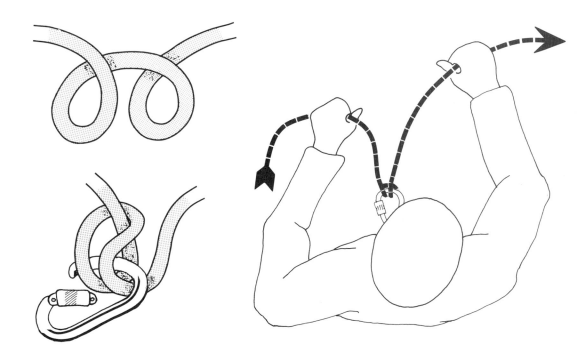

Fig 52   *Italian friction hitch belay. Clip a locking karabiner (preferably of the HMS type) into the waist tie. Now form the hitch as shown and clip it into the karabiner. Rope may now be paid out or drawn in simply by feeding rope through the hitch. Note that the hitch will, disconcertingly, rotate and resettle whenever you change the direction of feed – this is normal. If a fall occurs, grip the rope with the 'braking' hand (left in the diagram).*

Rope Care

Nylon climbing ropes are resistant to rotting but are subject to other kinds of damage. Careful use and storage will maintain rope strength and extend their useful life. Ropes suffer three kinds of traumatic damage during severe falls: melting, cutting and stress.

The melting point of nylon is relatively low, well within the temperature reached when a loaded rope drags across a stationary one. Take extra care when using the waist belay that the leader's rope will not drag over the second's anchoring rope.

Sharp edges of rock can cut through a rope during a fall. Try to avoid running the rope over or around sharp blocks or allowing it to settle in narrow cracks.

Rope fibres are irreversibly stretched by a severe fall, losing their all-important capacity to absorb energy. Replacement is the only cure.

Ropes may also sustain damage at other times. Falling stones could damage interior fibres while leaving the outer ones unmarked. Rope uncoiled on a ledge is especially vulnerable. If you suspect damage run the rope slowly between fingertips to check for irregularities.

Embedded grit cuts through interior fibres every time the rope is compressed. Grit can be removed by rinsing in lukewarm water, after which the rope is hung to dry in loose hanks away from direct heat; but it is still good practice never to stand on the rope.

In winter the sharp cutting edges of ice-axe and crampons come into close proximity to the rope. That cannot be avoided, but be careful not to trail the rope near your feet when walking in crampons.

Outer fibres abrade during normal use: the rope, once smooth and shiny, becomes furry. In itself this is not worrying, though indicative of general deterioration.

Some chemicals attack nylon. Investigations of broken ropes often reveal contamination by battery acid as the cause. Exposure to sunlight can have a similar effect in the long term.

The need for rope care extends to transit and storage. A rope is best stored in a dark, well-ventilated place not subject to direct heat. Obviously climbing ropes must not be used for purposes such as towing or securing luggage to a roof-rack, but there are also more subtle precautions to be taken. Neat coils trap kinks within the rope. It is better to allow coils to assume the more natural figure-of-eight shape. Occasionally dragging the rope over grass, or hanging it over a vertical drop, also helps to remove kinks.

A rope bought for scrambling or winter walking is little used and spends most of its time in the rucksack. Nevertheless it will at some time come to the end of its useful life. Unfortunately there is no reliable means of assessing precisely when that is. As a rough guide, and unless subject to damage from any of the causes listed above (in which case it should be retired immediately), make a point of replacing the rope within five years. If you find yourself using it regularly consider replacement within three years or less.

Coiling a Rope

Fig 53 Form coils from rope drawn out with the full spread of the arms.

Fig 54 Resist putting a twist into the rope and allow coils to fall into a natural 8 shape.

Fig 55 (Opposite top) When coiling is complete, double back the starting end and bind the finishing end around this and all other coils.

Fig 56 (Opposite bottom) Finally, tuck the finishing end through the loop thus formed and pull the starting end to secure.

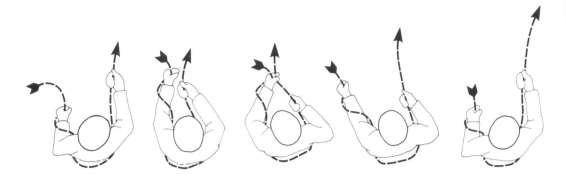

Fig 57   *Waist belaying (from left to right). The belayer is paying
out rope to his partner in the direction of the arrow.
Note that neither hand uncurls completely from the
rope at any time (the procedure for taking in rope
is similar). The twist of the rope at the wrist is
always around the hand (the 'braking' hand) which
is nearest the 'dead' rope piled on the ledge and not the
hand which directs the 'live' rope to the person
scrambling. If a fall occurs, the 'twist' arm (left
arm in the diagram) is rapidly swung across the
stomach and tensed. The action is almost instinctive.*

Procedure for Rope Protected Scrambling

Fig 58   *The rope has been uncoiled on a
broad ledge and now the leader
and second are tying on.*

Fig 59   *The second anchors his rope by
looping it over a large spike.*

Fig 60   The second, now anchored, belays
          the leader who scrambles to a ledge
          above the 'pitch'.

Fig 61   The leader has anchored to a spike
          and belays the rope while the
          second removes his own anchor loop.

Fig 62   The second scrambles up the pitch
          while belayed by the leader.

Fig 63   The leader continues to belay the
          second, who is now judging if it is
          safe for them to untie and proceed
          unroped.

COMMUNICATION

Few communication problems arise when scrambling because the distance between belay ledges (the *pitch*) is limited by the short rope. Your intentions can be conveyed informally. If, however, the ledges are not in direct vision, or if wind noise interferes, only a set of prearranged signals will prevent misunderstanding. Those adopted by rock climbers are suitably succinct:

Leader (already secured): 'Taking in!'
　Second releases the belayed rope. Leader pulls up remaining rope until it becomes tight.
Second: 'That's me!'
　Leader adopts belay position.
Leader: 'Climb when you're ready!'
　Second removes anchor.
Second: 'Climbing!'
　Leader takes in rope as second climbs.

Three other calls from the climber's vocabulary are useful to the second in instructing the belayed leader: 'slack!' (let out some rope); 'take in!' (pull in some rope); and 'tight!' (pull the rope tight). This last term indicates that you are about to fall off and will need all the help you can get.

FIXING RUNNERS
(Figs 64 & 65)

Runners are intermediate anchors placed by the leader in the hope of reducing the length of a fall. A tape sling is simply looped over an anchor point – it could be a flake of rock or a tree – and linked to the climbing rope by means of a karabiner. As the leader continues, the rope slides freely through this karabiner which, in the event of a fall, will serve as a pulley. The fall distance will then

Fig 64　*A tape runner. Note that the karabiner has been rotated so that its gate is positioned away from the rock.*

be limited to twice the distance above the runner, instead of twice the distance above the starting ledge.

Clearly this shorter fall will expose the leader to fewer injuries, but there are also benefits for the second and for the belay system as a whole. Not only will the strain of arresting a fall be less intense (because some energy is absorbed by the runner karabiner) but also less prolonged. The net effect is that the second is more likely to remain in control, and thus – in turn – will impose less strain on the main anchor.

The second collects the sling runner when following the pitch. The most con-

*Fig 65   An improvised runner using the
main rope.*

pulley may limit a nasty pendulum swing if
either leader or second were to fall.

The same improvisation may be extended
to provide basic security on ridge traverses.
Here both leader and second move simul-
taneously while the shortened rope that
links them drags between and around the
teeth of the ridge. The technique, simply
called *moving together*, is frequently used by
Alpinists in order to save time. Needless to
say the method will not tolerate abuse.

ABSEILING

Abseiling offers a convenient but hazardous
means of retreat down a difficult pitch. It

*Fig 66   Abseil practice. Extra precautions
may be taken when practising
abseil technique: note the helmets,
back-up anchors, and the belayer
feeding out a safety rope.*

venient means of carrying it (having first
unclipped its karabiner from the main rope)
is over the neck and one shoulder like a
bandoleer. Long slings are doubled up for
convenience, the karabiner then being clipped into both loops. To avoid later losing
the karabiner, impart a single twist in the
sling (forming an 8 shape) before drawing
the two loops together.

Runner placement is an art worth cul-
tivating. Even with such rudimentary
equipment as two tape slings it may be
possible to safely negotiate an otherwise
dangerous passage. Much can be achieved
by improvising with the main rope alone:
when trailed behind a block while crossing a
gully, for instance, the rope and its crude

would almost always be better to find another way down, or even to climb down the pitch conventionally (safeguarded by the normal belay procedure in reverse). But the day may come when no other alternative presents itself. Unlike in roped climbing when your weight is taken by sensitive hands and feet, body support while abseiling is entirely mechanical. Your life is trusted to a crude anchor and your clumsy grip of the rope. Moreover, when scrambling you are unlikely to have access to the equipment needed to arrange a safety rope or back-up anchor (although it is wise to employ these when practising the technique). When abseiling there is absolutely no room for error, no second chance.

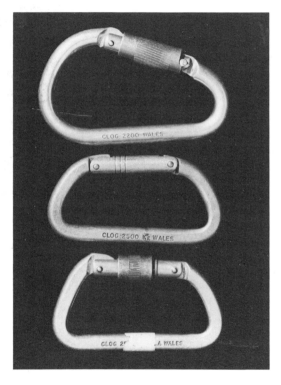

Fig 67   Karabiners. From top to bottom: HMS, ordinary, locking.

Tape Slings and Karabiners

In theory it should be possible to protect all scrambling pitches using the main rope alone, but on occasions it would be more convenient to form anchors using separate loops of rope.

In practice these slings are more useful in tape form. The following is a typical selection: two stitched tape slings of length 2.4m and width 25mm (these could also be used as sit-slings when abseiling); and two stitched tape slings of length 1.2m and width 25mm. The tape is no ordinary kind and the stitching not a do-it-yourself task, so visit a specialist climbing shop for these purchases.

Slings are linked to the main rope by karabiner clips. You will need the following: two locking karabiners rated at 2,500kg or greater (these are used in conjunction with the longer tapes); and two ordinary karabiners rated at 2,200kg or greater (for the shorter tapes). If you want to use the Italian friction hitch method of belaying the best locking karabiners to buy are those designated HMS and fitted with self-locking gates.

(Above) Glencoe – Gearr Aonach
(centre left) and Aonach
Dubh (right).

(Below) A narrow ledge solves a
problem on the Aonach
Eagach Ridge, Glencoe.

(*Above*) *On Carn Mor Dearg.*
Ben Nevis above the
cloud.

(*Right*) *Carn Mor Dearg. Deep*
powder on the ridge
towards Aonach Beag.

(*Left*) *Glen Etive.*

(Above)   Scafell Pinnacle with Great Gable in the background.

(Left)   Great Gable from Great End.

(Above)   Ascent to Y Garn, North Wales.

(Left)   Langdale, Lake District.

(Above)   *Snowdon South Ridge.*

(Below)   *Y Garn and the Ogwen Valley.*

Emergency Abseil Procedure with Basic Equipment

Fig 68   *(Above left) Select a firm anchor from which the rope cannot lift off, and arrange the middle of the rope securely around it.*

Fig 69   *(Above right) Tie a bulky knot at the rope ends to prevent you from inadvertently sliding off the rope.*

Fig 70   *(Left) Feed the knot down the pitch and check that it reaches the ledge.*

Fig 71   (*Above left*) *Arrange the rope for the classic abseil (as shown). Draw the rope between the legs, around the upper left thigh, diagonally across the chest, over the right shoulder, under the armpit, and into the left hand. You may reverse left and right as preferred.*

Fig 72   (*Above right*) *Walk slowly backwards over the edge, crouching low if an upright position might tend to lift the rope off its anchor point, and continue down the pitch. Note the body position and the spread of the legs. The grip of the lower hand governs braking, while the upper hand merely aids balance. The braking arm may be drawn across the chest to increase the braking effect.*

Fig 73   (*Left*) *After untying the bulky knot, pull down one end to retrieve the rope. Watch out for loose stones which the rope may dislodge.*

Setting up the Abseil

The first task is to find a suitable anchor point. These are some of the important features to look for:

1. Firmness (for obvious reasons).
2. A position somewhere high above the ledge (two metres or more) to prevent the rope rolling off at the start of the descent.
3. A secure lodging for the rope so there is no chance it will shift position under load.
4. Absence of narrow cracks or other constrictions which could jam the rope during retrieval.
5. Absence of sharp edges which might cut into the rope when your weight is applied.

If you are carrying tape slings it might be better to place one over the anchor and thread the abseil rope through that. This small sacrifice helps ensure easy retrieval of the rope. Note that the direct nylon to nylon contact is acceptable in this case because both components remain stationary, at least until rope retrieval when some fusing will occur (a good reason not to trust slings you find discarded).

The next job is to find the middle of the abseil rope and arrange this securely over or around the anchor point (or pull one end through the tape sling until the middle is reached). Now tie a bulky knot at the two ends – to prevent you inadvertently sliding off the end of the rope – and feed them over the edge. You will want to check that they reach the next ledge! The abseil is now set up.

Abseil Descent

There are two basic methods of sliding down an abseil rope. The first, the *classic* abseil, requires no special equipment, simply using the rope arranged around the body. Friction generated between rope and clothing helps to limit the rate of descent. Even over thick clothing this causes some discomfort, so clearly this is no time to be wearing shorts and T-shirt.

The second method is more complicated but a lot less painful. First, leg loops are improvised from one of the 2.4m tapes and linked by a locking karabiner. Next the abseil rope is formed into an Italian friction hitch and clipped into the locking karabiner.

In both methods the grip of the lower (braking) hand regulates the rate of descent, which is why it is advisable to wear gloves.

You are now ready to go. After a final check of the anchor and knots, walk smoothly backwards over the edge and down the rock with no jolts or jumps. The most stable position is with the feet flat against the rock and legs spread apart to form a triangle. The legs and lower part of the body are roughly at right angles to the rock while the upper part curves more upright. The bold posture is not to impress onlookers but to maintain balance. This is especially important if the descent is a diagonal one, otherwise you may pendulum across the rocks with risk of injury and of losing your grip on the rope.

Descent technique needs to be practised under controlled conditions (i.e. with a safety rope and back-up anchor) before it begins to feel natural. Take special care when moving over the edge – the most vulnerable moment – to ensure that the abseil rope does not lift off its anchor. If necessary crouch down to keep the ropes low and then carefully creep over the edge.

Italian Friction Hitch Abseil

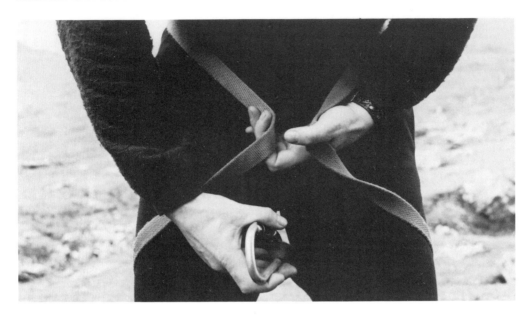

Fig 74   *Form a sit sling as shown using a long tape sling and locking karabiner. The karabiner links three tape loops: two drawn around the hips and one between the legs.*

Fig 75   *Form an Italian friction hitch in the locking karabiner.*

Retrieving the Rope

Before the last person descends you will want to know if the rope can indeed be easily retrieved. A short test pull will verify this. If the test fails then the anchor will need to be rearranged. All being well, after everyone has regrouped on the lower ledge it should be a simple matter to pull down on one end and retrieve the rope. Beware of falling rocks that the snaking rope end may have dislodged.

Sometimes, despite all precautions, the rope will jam after the last person has descended. First check that no twists have developed near the anchor point, by separating the two ends and flicking them away from the rock. If the rope still refuses to move, scramble a few metres up to one side to facilitate a pull from a different angle. If that also fails you may be forced to abandon the rope until you can return with more equipment. If you need the rope in order to complete the descent, however, then your position becomes very serious indeed, although with care it is extremely unlikely that it will come to this. Whatever happens, resist all temptation to swarm hand over hand up the rope, which can be very dangerous if you tire or if the rope suddenly frees itself.

Prusiking is the only reliable means of reascending jammed abseil ropes. The technique, in which prusik knots are tied around both ropes, is a specialised emergency procedure occasionally used in rock climbing and Alpine mountaineering. If you think you may need to know the method – for instance if you are contemplating Via Ferrata scrambles in the Dolomites – then consult one of the technical texts suggested in the bibliography.

WINTER WALKING

Fig 76 Carneddau in winter. The ridge between Carnedd Llewelyn
and Pen Yr Helgi Du.

9 The Mountains in Winter

Thoughts of winter evoke grey images of pluming breath and clinging mist, of companions' faces drawn tight and cheerless by a Siberian wind. Winter, we might think, is the sullen interlude between two glorious seasons, but from creeping miseries of cold and discomfort emerges ecstasy. The sensation is unique, and the search for it brings us again and again to the snow-covered hills.

WHERE TO GO

Good snow conditions are rare in Britain. Typically snow falls during cold northerlies, lying as deep powder until a week of warm westerlies reduces it to slush. Sparse remains are then frozen into icy patches until the next fall of powder. For this reason the best walking is often found when the hills are under a light snow cover but when boggy ground is frozen; or alternatively, but more rarely, when deep snow has consolidated into a firm layer. The most tiring and dangerous conditions are found immediately after a heavy snowfall or after freezing rain.

The three most popular mountain regions for summer walking also provide the main interest in winter. Often the less dramatic mountain groups among these regions give most enjoyment. In North Wales, for instance, the broad topped Carneddau hills offer more continuity than the neighbouring boulder-strewn Glyders.

An important consideration is the choice of base. Camping can be thoroughly miserable if you have no means of drying clothes from one day to the next. In bad weather there is a good chance you will spend most of your precious holiday in a launderette. A better alternative might be to stay in a bunkhouse or hostel.

WEATHER

In Britain no regular annual pattern of winter weather asserts itself year after year as it often does on the Continent. Instead we are subjected to wild fluctuations between bitter northeasterlies, mild southwesterlies, and all points between. Nevertheless, certain weather regimes – periods from a few days to three or four weeks – are known to establish themselves at some time during the winter. Their significance is all the greater because winter terrain is preconditioned by days or weeks of snowfall, wind and temperature changes. Most of what you encounter on your walk is history. Common weather regimes fall under one of three broad categories: mild, freeze/thaw and cold.

Mild

A train of depressions arriving from the Atlantic often initiates a mild regime when

Fig 77   Powder snow on the Carneddau.

warm, moist winds drawn up from the south-west quickly dispose of snow lying on open slopes. Mild periods frequently dominate the weather during December or early January, perhaps completely stripping mountains south of Scotland of their early snow. In these conditions walking loses its winter character and assumes that of miserable summer weather.

The regime may also develop later in the season when snow cover is deeper. Although the snow may by then be able to withstand its influence, conditions will be extremely unpleasant while it prevails. The reasons are fairly obvious: mild weather is often preceded by a heavy fall of snow, and it will be through this thawing mass that you will have to wade.

More worryingly, if the new snowfall covers icy snow then conditions are ripe for avalanche – both during the snowstorm and the first day or two of thaw. Temperature rises may also trigger the collapse of existing but unstable snow features such as cornices.

Freeze/Thaw

Snow responds to fluctuating temperatures by alternately freezing and thawing. The frequency of the alternation may be anything from a few hours to a few days, but the overall effect is that lying snow gradually packs down into a more favourable consistency.

The short freeze/thaw cycle is simply a sequence of cold nights following warm days. Typically this occurs during fine weather late in the season. In the morning the snow will be hard and reliable (crampons may be necessary), but during the day – and especially on south facing slopes – the snow layer quickly softens until it will no longer support your weight. It follows that an early start makes the best of the conditions.

Lengthy freeze/thaw cycles make up the typical mix of winter weather: neither particularly good nor especially bad. Typically a northwesterly wind will bring a day of snow, followed by a day of sleet or rain, followed by a day of hail showers and occasional sunshine: all very variable and unpredictable. Precisely what the overall effect will be depends very much on the time of year and the state of preceding conditions. In December, for instance, the weather pattern might lightly cover the hills in snow one day and all but remove it the next; whereas in midwinter a deposit of hail may become sandwiched between a layer of icy snow and a surface layer of new powder – an intractable and potentially dangerous combination. Conditions encountered during a freeze/thaw cycle vary tremendously according to altitude. You may quit a spring-like valley only to climb up into arctic conditions at a thousand metres.

Cold

Cold regimes are often associated with re-silient areas of high atmospheric pressure. High pressure systems are stable in meteorological terms, remaining stationary for perhaps three or four weeks. Under their influence a cold easterly airstream circles across the country, lowering temperatures to sub-zero both night and day.

The absence of a daytime thaw means

Fig 78   Bad conditions on Bristly Ridge, Glyder Fach

that existing cover never enters a freeze/thaw cycle and lies throughout as an un-supportive powder. Strong winds scour this powder from exposed slopes and ridges, depositing it as deep drifts on the lee slopes and in valleys. A route chosen with care – perhaps along a series of linking ridges – will make the best of this opportunity, enjoying the good weather and spectacular scenery without suffering the inconvenience of deep, unconsolidated snow.

Tremendous accumulations of water ice accompany a prolonged cold regime. Frozen drainage water will present an obvious but formidable obstacle where it flows across an otherwise easy path, often quite low down on the mountain. More treacherous are the smaller flows which lie concealed beneath fresh falls of snow at higher altitudes.

GROUND CONDITIONS

The complexity of mountain weather and topography guarantee that you will encounter a wide variety of conditions during the day. Some of those most commonly met are summarised below.

Verglas

A thin transparent coating of ice, verglas forms over rocks which have cooled and are then exposed to moist air. Verglassed rocks simply look damp but prove to be extremely slippery. There may be no alternative but to fit crampons. A particularly unpleasant variant goes by the name of *frozen rain*. Formed when rain falls on to cold rock, it can accumulate to a thickness of a centimetre or more. Either of these conditions may occur in the absence of snow, which helps explain why people are so often caught unprepared.

Iced Rocks

Winds soon remove most of the snow cover from rock ridges. If, in addition, daytime temperatures exceed zero the warmed rocks will begin to protrude from among remaining patches of snow as the route reasserts its summer character.

At other times the rocks of a ridge may be plated in snow-ice or rime deposits (sometimes called *fog crystals* or *atmospheric icing*). Both conditions obscure the true features of the rock and demand a cautious approach in crampons.

Water Ice

All forms of surface water – streams, snow melt, hillside drainage – will eventually freeze into ice flows during a prolonged cold spell. The scale of these flows can vary from a single step where the path crosses the bed of a small gully, to hundreds of metres where it follows a stream course. Whenever fresh or drifted snow overlies water ice the problems are compounded.

It is not possible to kick a step into water ice. If the ice is almost level you may be able to teeter along it as you would a frozen pavement (instep crampons can help here); but if the ice flow slopes, or if the path narrows and there is a drop below, you may be left with no option but to fit crampons.

Another possibility is to cut footholds with the ice-axe. However, more than a few metres of step cutting in water ice is extremely laborious and the result is rarely satisfactory – especially since a slip could not be checked with the axe which would merely bounce off the hard surface. If crampons are not being used you may decide to protect the crossing with a rope.

Powder Snow

Powder snow is usually freshly fallen, although during periods of very cold weather it may be several days old. By definition it lacks substance, making for tiresome walking. The axe shaft will offer little extra support, and *self-arrest* (*see* Chapter 12) will be ineffective if you do slip.

Where powder snow overlies an ice layer the steps are especially prone to collapse. For that matter, so is the entire slope. Powder snow which overlies a ridge crest is no more helpful, simply slithering from beneath your feet and yet without revealing

Fig 79   Snowdon Horseshoe. Perfect snow conditions on Crib Y Ddysgl.

footholds on the rock itself.

Wind tends to strip open slopes of powder, reforming it into deep drifts on lee slopes and in the beds of streams and gullies. Wind action also produces the beautiful snow sculptures which overhang lake shores, streams and gully exits. These *cornices* are the poisonous mushrooms of the winter garden. They are difficult to detect from above; walkers who venture out on to their rims remain oblivious to danger until the moment of collapse. The fracture line of cornices is many metres back from the rim, so give them a wide berth and beware of following careless footsteps near the edge.

Windslab

Wind-blown powder eventually compacts into more or less cohesive slabs overlying a substratum of loose snow. On relatively level ground, and provided it is of sufficient thickness, windslab offers a firm footing and speeds progress. On steeper slopes, when it is necessary to kick into the crust, it breaks away in tell-tale blocks and leaves your feet floundering for support in the loose powder beneath. The axe shaft is similarly un-supported, although the pick may have sufficient grip on the crust to arrest a slide if necessary. The accompanying and very real risk of avalanche adds to the anxiety.

Wet Snow

Snow can exhibit various degrees of wet-ness. New snow undergoing a rapid thaw offers no support to feet or axe; whereas old snow, on the borderline between freez-ing and melting, sometimes achieves the ideal consistency for kicking steps.

Wet snow is a prerequisite for really good conditions to develop, but has little to recommend it in itself. Boots and clothing become quickly saturated, and it can feel a lot colder and more unpleasant than on days when lower temperatures are recorded. Old snow becomes wet under the influence of warmer daytime temperatures, so that what in the morning was a crisp coat is transformed into a sodden blanket by the afternoon. Nevertheless, an axe shaft thrust deep may penetrate through to the firmer part of the layer and offer some security.

Crusty Snow

Wet snow develops a crust after night-time frosts. The thickness of this crust will

Fig 80   The Great Ridge of the Carneddau. Arctic conditions on Drum.

dictate the character of the walk. If it is very thin it can be ignored and everything depends on the consistency of the underlying snow. If it is thick (more than a few centimetres) then not only will it support your weight on level ground, but it will respond to a penetrating kick on steeper slopes. These are ideal walking conditions.

Unfortunately the dividing line between a supportive crust and one which cruelly breaks under your weight is a very fine one indeed. Quite apart from the extra effort and delay, the hard edges of the broken crust eventually bruise the ankles. It is like spending a day stepping in and out of chimney pots.

Snow-ice

Snow-ice is the product of repeated freezing and thawing. By definition it is old snow, and as such may be overlain by more recent falls. When exposed and in its frozen state, it is the most predictable and reliable of all snow conditions. It responds extremely well to crampons but not to step kicking. The spike or pick of the axe will be firmly held by the snow, but the shaft will not penetrate. A self-arrest ought to be successful if applied quickly, but not if the surface is particularly icy or if there is any delay in applying the brake. Later in the day, especially on south facing slopes, the snow-ice surface enters the thaw phase of its cycle and takes on the characteristics of wet snow.

Ice

Ice – in this context an advanced state of snow-ice as opposed to water ice – is occasionally found in patches late in the season, when it is usually avoidable, but it can also form mid-season in huge sheets, often on south facing slopes. Notorious examples are the south-east flanks of Ben Nevis and Snowdon. Crampons are necessary, and opportunities for applying self-arrest are minimal. The condition is treacherous because in summer these are simple paths, and the winter difficulties are frequently underestimated.

SNOW AVALANCHES

Certain notorious slopes in the Alps regularly avalanche. Guidebooks contain references to them, sometimes indicating a time of day after which the slopes will be unsafe to cross. Some mountains are climbed almost entirely in the hours of darkness in an attempt to minimise the risk.

Avalanches are thankfully much less of a problem in Britain. We have smaller mountains, less snow and more rapid stabilisation. Winter climbers are most at risk because their sport takes them into avalanche-prone features such as snow gullies, although walkers are by no means immune. But just how great is the risk? My experience is that sizeable avalanches – seen or heard – are rare. The statistics bear this out. However, the fact that avalanches can be unleashed by our own perforating footsteps is reason enough for constant vigilance. The trick is

---

Avalanches: Precautions

Avoid Periods of High Risk
- During heavy snowfall
- During the two day settling period after heavy snow
- After a sudden rise in temperature
- During and after heavy rain

Avoid Places of High Risk
- Lee slopes (deep snow and/or windslab surface layer)
- Slopes of gradients 30–45 degrees
- Corniced rims (keep well back)
- Approaches overhung by cornices
- Gully approaches
- Convex slopes
- Slopes known to overlie rock slabs or grass

Warning Signals
- Evidence of previous avalanches or smaller snow slides
- Hollow sounding crust
- Collapsing crust
- Pieces of crust sliding away below footsteps
- Cracks in snow surface
- Evidence of melting

The Axe Test
Progressively prod through the surface layers with the axe shaft to detect layers and assess risk. If sudden variations in resistance are sensed dig a pit face to reveal the evidence. Watch out for:

- Windslab layer on powder snow base
- Windslab layer on hard base
- Wet snow layer on hard base
- Any discontinuity between layers (air-gap, layer of hailstones, etc.)

More Information
Refer to the bibliography for comprehensive texts on avalanches.

not to be caught in the wrong place at the wrong time. To achieve that, not surprisingly, we need to recognise wrong places and wrong times.

Snow will avalanche when the underlying surface can no longer sustain the burden. This might be because of increased layer weight (from additional snowfall or your own body weight); decreased adhesion (melting or rain drainage at the interface of two layers); disintegration of the layer (perhaps initiated by cornice collapse from above); or, more likely, some combination of the three. Some slopes are also more vulnerable than others, either because of the nature of underlying terrain (shelving rock, grass, convex gradient), or because of particular snow conditions (fresh snow, wet snow, windslab).

With the help of physics and a little imagination we can now see why windslab overlying hail on a lee slope should break away from a walker's destabilising footsteps; or why thawing fresh snow should

---

Avalanches: What to do if Caught

The odds of surviving an avalanche are not good. Adopting the suggestions which follow might just tip the balance in your favour.

Precautions
If *forced* to cross a slope which may avalanche, do so one at a time in a diagonal descent, avoiding convex gradients, and take these precautions:

- Remove axe wrist loop
- Unclip rucksack waistbelt
- Fasten clothing/hood/gloves

If roped, the belayer unties so that both will not be dragged down by a big avalanche and belays from a 'safe' place on the slope, for example a rock outcrop.

What to do if Avalanched
If the slope begins to slide:

- Thrust in the axe shaft and hold on tight

If carried away:

- Make for the edge if you can by rolling or even 'swimming'

- Try not to gasp for air (and so inhale powder)

In the final seconds of the slide:

- Struggle to break surface
- Create an air gap around your face

What to do if your Partners are Avalanched
Watch their progress down the slope and then:

- Go and mark the point where they were avalanched
- Descend and mark the point where they were last seen
- Quickly call (not go) for the assistance of people nearby
- Look for signs of clothing, axe, rope, and so on
- Search the likely place of burial by probing with axe
- Ask others to go for help (*see* Chapter 15)
- Continue search until help arrives
- If alone, search for up to an hour before going for help

cascade from a hillside clad in rock slabs which shelve like the tiles of a roof. Or why a cornice, weakened by a mild south-westerly and overburdened by the petulant walker stamping on its brow, should finally crack and groan and shove off for the valley.

ROUTES

Route Planning

Which, then, are the good winter walks would be impossible to say. The list would change from week to week, or perhaps day to day. A good route, wherever it may be, is simply one which makes the best of the prevailing weather and snow conditions. There are nevertheless some obvious candidates. After heavy snow, for instance, broad ridge crests raked by wind invariably make better approaches to the summits than intervening and drift-choked corries.

The ability to previsualise topography from contour lines is no less of a valuable aid to route planning in winter than it is in summer, except that now the image will be modified by what you can deduce about the snow overlay – icy and thin here, soft and deep there, and so on. This new picture will show you what can be reasonably attempted in the few hours of daylight.

Route Finding

Winter returns the landscape to its ancient state of wilderness. Paths, cairns and once familiar landmarks are progressively obscured by the white cloak. The art of route finding reverts to its purest, most instinctive form.

As in summer, route finding operates at one of three levels: immediate, local, and general. At the immediate level your concern might be dealing with an icy path or thinning snow cover; at a local level, negotiating a snow covered boulder field or corniced exit; and at the general level, locating the ridges least exposed to wind or those slopes least vulnerable to avalanche.

Winter intensifies not only the delights of hill walking but also the problems, the prime example being route finding in bad weather. On occasions you will be forced to rely totally on elaborate navigational techniques (Chapter 14). You may also be forced to rope up if winds are stirring the lying snow, because in these *white-out* conditions it can be impossible to distinguish between ground and sky, or even to discern objects at a distance of two metres – a chilling prospect in every sense of the word.

10 Equipment for Winter Walking

In winter we depend on equipment not only for comfort and survival but for progress. On difficult ground a steadying hand or well-placed foot is no longer enough; instead we need the more positive security of ice-axe and crampons. Our clothing, already juggling to balance comfort through sun and rain, must now protect against bitter winds and driving snow.

BASIC EQUIPMENT

Basic equipment used in summer walking forms the central core of what is required in winter. For that reason the following merely supplements the itemised headings of Chapter 2.

Clothing

Legwear

Medium weight breeches insulate adequately well, supplemented by long johns if necessary, although the gap in clothing which inevitably develops at the waist will be wickedly exploited by penetrating cold. Salopettes solve that problem with a bib-and-brace design.

Gaiters prevent snow from entering boots at the ankle and at the same time windproof exposed stockings. A zip at rear or, better, front allows fitting or removal at any time during the day without first having to remove boots. Although it is as well to fit them from the outset because zips are invariably awkward to fasten with cold fingers.

Underwear

The basic function of underwear is to buffer the hot/cold fluctuation experienced during typically erratic movement (i.e. bouts of hard uphill walking followed by short rests). So-called thermal underwear achieves this by stilling the air at the skin surface and by transferring sweat to the outer clothing layers. Polypropylene is a popular choice, although other materials – wool among them – can claim their own advantages.

The importance of stabilising temperature variations in the trunk region means that a long-sleeved vest in one or other of the thermal materials is the single most valuable item of underwear. The role of long johns is less crucial, although they are useful in upgrading summer weight breeches to a winter standard.

Midwear

Extra pullovers are sufficient for adding insulation at rest stops, although some form of padded and zip-fronted jacket would be more convenient. Full specification duvets are inappropriate for this purpose; instead a simple lightweight jacket with synthetic fill will be more versatile and compact, and will also double as the main item of emergency clothing.

Outerwear

Wind and waterproof outer layers correspond to those used in summer. A heavier jacket is not such a handicap now because fittings such as drawcord, sealed cuffs and wired hood will substantially increase the overall efficiency of the clothing system.

Nylon overtrousers protect clothing from saturation when glissading, practising ice-axe self-arrest and digging snow holes. Worn at other times they would contribute alarmingly to the speed of a slide. Nylon waterproof jackets have a similar effect. Windproofing outerwear for both trunk and legs is therefore better provided for in a natural or heavily textured synthetic material.

Hand/Headwear

Ski-hats and simple bob-caps are inadequate in severe conditions unless combined with a thermal Balaclava. Otherwise a full Balaclava in wool or synthetic fibre would be better. Some designs convert into a hat shape to reduce overheating during the ascent.

Gloves and Balaclavas in a thermal material play a slightly different role from thermal underwear, actually becoming part of a miniature system of layered insulation for the extremities. Inner gloves, for instance, add to overall hand warmth in combination with a full mitt. They are also useful when worn by themselves during approaches, or for maintaining basic protection from the cold while fastening crampons or performing other intricate tasks.

Equipment Checklist (winter)

Boots
Long socks
Short socks
Gaiters
Long johns
Breeches/salopettes
Thermal undershirt
Midwear (pullover)
Windproof jacket
Waterproof jacket
Inner gloves
Mitts
Thermal Balaclava
Balaclava
Goggles, sunglasses

Ice-axe
Crampons
Rope

Spare pullovers (2)/insulated jacket
Spare socks
Spare mitts
Spare hat
Waterproof overtrousers
Light sleeping bag (one among group)
Small foam mat
Map
Compass
Whistle
Headtorch
Spare torch battery and bulbs
Food and drink
First-aid kit
Survival bag
Rucksack

Choice of handwear raises many dilemmas. Ideally a single pair of gloves or mitts should insulate, windproof and waterproof your hands without loss of dexterity. In practice this never happens and those three requirements must be built from separate layers each having a distinct function.

Thermal inner gloves offer basic protection without loss of sensitivity. On top of those, mitts in wool or fibre pile (long cuffs) provide the main insulation. In most circumstances that combination alone will suffice, because both wool and fibre pile are good insulators when wet. Overmitts will add to the level of protection but are unlikely to remain waterproof (if ever they were) for very long. Moreover, a three-way combination such as this integrates badly and results in poor sensitivity. A better alternative might be to carry medium thickness gloves as emergency spares. According to conditions these could then partner either the mitts or the thermal inners.

Emergency and Ancillary Equipment

Spare hat and mitts supplement existing clothing during periods of severe cold (and replace those lost to a sudden gust of wind), but there is little point in merely duplicating normal wear. Consider instead carrying something which will bring versatility to the existing system.

A spare pair of stockings soothes feet and tempers if you are unlucky enough to break through to a stream in the early stages of a walk. At times they could double as emergency mitts if it transpires (as it so often does) that others in the group are not so well equipped.

As already noted, an insulated jacket (or a couple of thick pullovers) constitutes the main item of spare clothing. In addition a light sleeping bag among the party makes good disaster insurance if someone is immobilised by hypothermia or injury.

Some rucksack backs are padded with a removable foam pad, which will provide valuable ground insulation in an emergency. Otherwise consider buying a short foam sleeping mat. This is most conveniently carried as a loose roll lining the main rucksack compartment.

Winter conditions are so unpredictable that a rope ought to be regarded as essential equipment. It need not be a full length climbing rope, and the type specified in Chapter 8 would be suitable.

First-aid kit and survival equipment remain as for summer. However, a simple handtorch is now inadequate for those occasions (not uncommon in winter) when you are overtaken by nightfall. Instead a good quality headtorch will leave both hands free to use an ice-axe or consult the map. Cheap models tend to be unreliable, dim and short-lived. The best ones, made from nylon or other durable plastic, are powered by long-life batteries mounted inside a rainproof box on the rear of the headband. A torch of this type, though expensive, is well worth the investment. The torch itself should be kept fairly accessible, whereas the spare bulbs and battery are better packed along with the other small emergency items.

Sunglasses are able to reduce glare from the snow, but goggles are more efficient at shielding the eyes from stinging hail or spindrift. Condensation will be a problem, however, unless these are well vented. Breakages are inevitable, so cheap versions must suffice.

Food and drink requirements are quite different in winter. A flask of hot drink between two might be considered a luxury in an otherwise lightweight pack, but the psychological uplift more than compensates. For some reason hot fruit juice seems

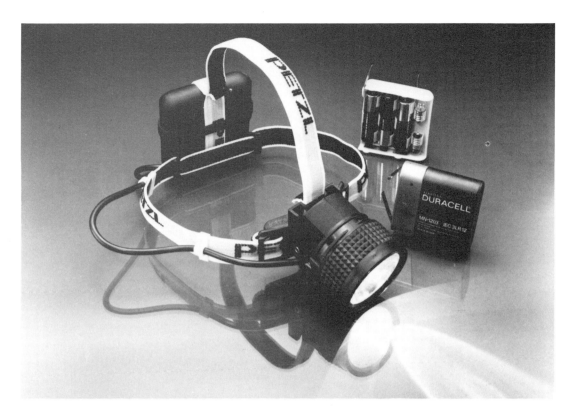

Fig 81   A durable and efficient headtorch (Petzl Zoom).

more therapeutic than tea or coffee. The powdered variety guarantees the hottest brew.

Sandwiches freeze into inedible rectangles, whereas fruit is either too cold to eat or else too fiddly to peel. Nuts, dried fruit and chocolate are more convenient. Avoid thick chocolate bars in very cold weather if you fear for your teeth.

CHOOSING AN ICE-AXE
(Figs 82 & 83)

An ice-axe has many functions. In ordinary circumstances it merely aids balance as a glorified walking stick. On steeper slopes it serves as a mobile handhold for added security. While on the steepest ground it is used as an essential aid to progress, either by embedding the pick and pulling up on the shaft or else by chipping out a foothold with the adze. In exceptional circumstances it becomes an anchor around which to tie a rope, and in the last resort a brake with which to arrest an otherwise unstoppable slide. The design of a good walking axe reflects each of these functions.

Optimum shaft length will vary according to individual preference and physique and could be anything from 65 to 85cm. A useful first indicator is to hold the axe by your side (loosely, by the head), and check if the spike reaches to within a couple of

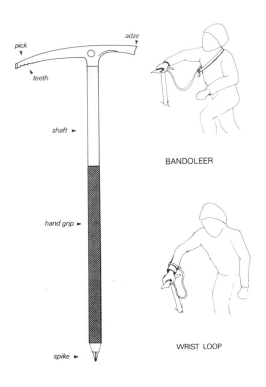

Fig 82   The main features of an ice-axe.
The axe may be secured by a wrist
loop or bandoleer attachment.

centimetres of the floor. A short axe is more manageable during self-arrest (the technique of using the axe to stop a slide), but a longer axe will have a better steadying effect and so make the slip – and therefore the need to self-arrest – that much less likely.

Metal shafts are strong and light. Unfortunately the bare or painted finish is both cold and slippery to handle. Look for an axe fitted with rubber hand grip.

The profile of the spike is more important than its actual sharpness. A slender, fluted taper seems the most efficient. Note that

any sort of lip at the ferrule, or bulbous end to the shaft, will severely hinder penetration in hard snow.

Some axe heads are forged, others are welded or riveted from sheet metal components. Each construction method has its own strengths and weaknesses, and there is no reason to suppose that one is intrinsically better than the other. It is more important that the head nestles comfortably in the hand and that curvature of the adze and pick follow a suitable profile.

Adzes come in all shapes and sizes. Inclined and shovel-shaped adzes have applications in ice climbing but are hopeless for cutting steps. Those gently curved in both planes seem to be the most efficient step cutters.

Hooked, inclined and S-shaped picks are designed specifically for steep climbing. In a walking axe look for gentle pick curvature. This will give adequate security on steep slopes without being too snatchy when applying the self-arrest brake. Teeth cut into the underside of the tip improve holding power, whereas those cut close to the shaft (for added security when climbing) merely shred mitts faster than otherwise.

Some sort of security loop is a good idea in case you drop the axe while engaged in crossing a ridge or steep slope. Opinions vary as to whether this should be in the form of a wrist loop or a line to a chest bandoleer. Indeed, some people question the wisdom of fitting any kind of security loop; the theory being that in a fall which is beyond control (such as when caught in an avalanche) the victim is best relieved of the flailing axe. While certainly true when practising self arrest, in general it is probably more important to prevent accidental loss of the axe.

Compared with the chest line, the wrist

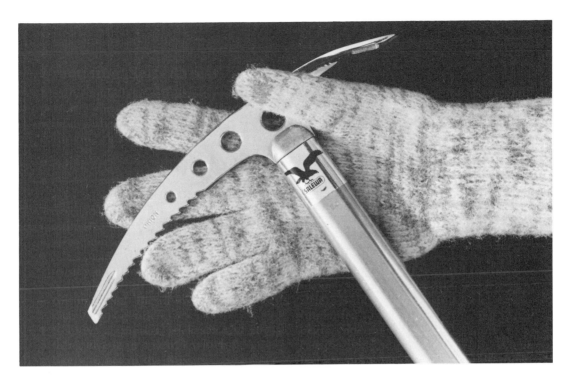

Fig 83   A good general purpose ice-axe.

loop is neater, more supportive during steep ascents and less likely to cause tripping. Its biggest drawback is the inconvenience of having to change it from hand to hand when zigzagging up a slope (the axe being held always on the uphill side). The answer is to try both and adopt the method you find most convenient.

Another breeding ground of conflicting theories is the sharpening of axes. Some sharpen adze, pick and spike with a fine-to-medium file before each outing; others never sharpen them. A policy somewhere between these two extremes seems wise. Depending on use, a walking axe should require sharpening no more than once or twice a year. When filing, follow existing bevels on both pick and adze. Spikes are better left slightly blunt (though not rounded) to minimise the likelihood of a piercing injury. Oil lightly smeared over exposed metal will prevent corrosion during storage.

The spikes and picks of ice-axes have a propensity for jabbing expensive car upholstery. It makes sense to detach axes from rucksacks during transit, although the only certain cure is to fit rubber head covers and spike bungs.

CHOOSING CRAMPONS
(Figs 84 to 86)

An ice-axe may stop a slide developing into a fall, but crampons might have prevented the slide in the first place. In other words, if conditions are such that you need an ice-axe

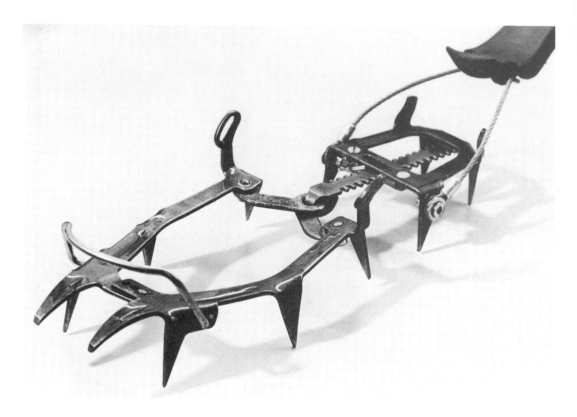

*Fig 84   A climbing crampon with quick-release 'step-in' binding
(Salewa 'Scissor').*

then there is every likelihood you will need crampons as well.

Basically there are three types of crampon: climbing, walking and instep. Climbing crampons have extra points which project forwards at the toe and are often fitted with quick-release clip bindings. Walking crampons are lighter and less cumbersome and may or may not have the projecting front points. They are usually flexible in length and are fitted to the boots using straps and buckles. Instep crampons are primarily intended for icy tracks rather than mountain paths. They have fewer points (usually four), all of which protrude downwards from a short baseplate. Instep

crampons are usually fastened to the boots with a single strap and buckle.

What type of crampon you choose depends very much on the kind of conditions you are likely to meet. If you wish to pursue winter walking to its limit only walking or climbing crampons will do. Otherwise a set of instep crampons make a useful emergency item for when autumn or spring weather turns unexpectedly wintry, or in dealing with low level paths plagued by ice flows.

Designs for full crampons are as many and as varied as those for ice-axes. Assuming you will want to avoid the numerous and exotic ice climbing crampons, the final

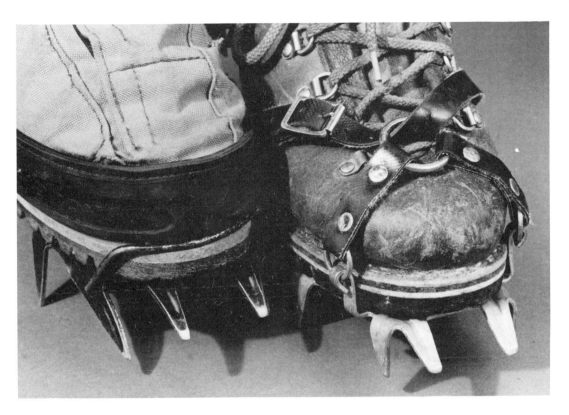

Fig 85   A general purpose walking/climbing crampon. The walking crampon (right) is fitted to a flexible soled winter walking boot using buckled straps. On the left a quick-release crampon is fitted to a rigid soled plastic boot which is protected by a 'Yeti' gaiter.

choice depends more on which model best fits your boots rather than on any intricacy of design. Every model will be adjustable for length, though not all are adjustable for width.

Quick-release, or *step-in*, bindings are kind to cold hands during fitting and removal. Unfortunately they work well only on rigid boots which have a pronounced lip at the toe and heel. The alternative means of crampon attachment is by buckled straps. Some crampons are sold complete with straps; for those which are not, straps can be bought in a do-it-yourself kit complete with soft rivets and explicit instructions.

When buying instep crampons it is important to check that the baseplate will positively locate against the boot heel and that sole width falls within the range of adjustment of the crampon.

The procedure for crampon care and protection is similar to that already indicated for ice-axes. In addition it is as well to check the tightness of adjusting nuts from time to time. A long, buckled strap makes a good standby on the mountain in case of

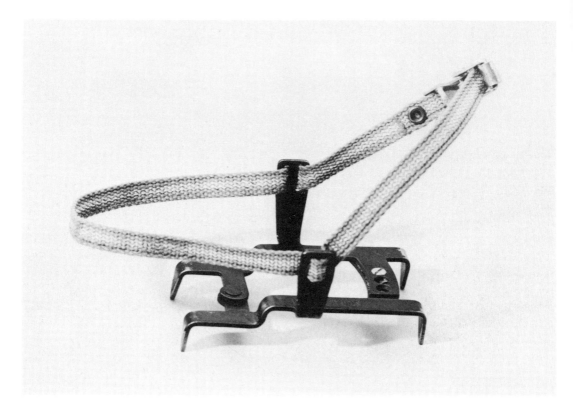

Fig 86   A width-adjustable instep crampon (Stubai Instep).

crampon or strap breakages, when it will be too cold for more elaborate running repairs.

Not all rucksacks are fitted with efficient exterior crampon carrying straps, and yet there is a risk to other equipment if crampons are carried inside. A detachable rucksack pocket or custom-made bag in tough nylon solves the problem.

11 Movement on Snow and Ice

The techniques of winter walking merge imperceptibly with those of snow and ice climbing. It is the difference in attitude which sets climber and walker apart: one deliberately seeks out difficulties, the other seeks to avoid them. But neither entirely succeeds and the difficulties are the same. Either way, the ability to move competently over snow and ice – easy or difficult – adds immeasurably to the safety and enjoyment of the day. If you can keep your feet when all about you are losing theirs . . .

OVER GENTLE TERRAIN

Winter walking mostly consists of following a beaten trail of compacted snow: the route will be obvious, the pace fast. If drifting is severe, however, or the route unfrequented, your pace will slow to a crawl.

Breaking trail through deep snow is a tiring and demoralising task, best shared evenly among the group. Rate of progress is disproportionately suppressed by an increase in slope angle. For instance, a 40 degree slope of deep powder, however short, may so impede progress that you are forced to turn back.

Moving over hard snow is altogether a different experience. On level ground it is simply a matter of strolling effortlessly across the surface, but where there is even a slight gradient you may need to kick steps for security – a good reason for having stiffish soles and firm uppers in your winter footwear. In direct ascent the action might be described as a punching swing from the knee; whereas when crossing a slope or ascending diagonally it is more of a slicing swing with the side of the boot. In either case the step ought to have a slight inward slope because only a relatively small proportion of the boot sole will be directly supported.

During descent, punch steps into firm snow using the heel. The action is not, as you might expect, the backward jab of a rugby player preparing a place kick, but simply an exaggerated and stiff-legged version of normal walking. Raising the toes sharpens the heel profile and improves the security of the step as a consequence. If, however, the snow is of very hard consistency, or interspersed with icy patches, it would be safer to fit crampons.

The ice-axe is not required to aid progress while step kicking on gentle slopes, but it *is* carried in readiness to correct a slip. Ascents and descents of steeper slopes are actively supported and secured by the axe (these are described later).

Holding the Axe

How you take hold of the ice-axe depends very much on what you hope to do with it. Of the several recognised hand positions, just three (and their variants) find regular use while winter walking. For convenience we might refer to these as the *support*, *brake* and *cutting* positions. Their common applications are as follows:

support   normal walking
crossing a slope
diagonal ascent/descent
direct ascent/descent

brake   crossing a steep slope
diagonal steep ascent/
    descent
self-arrest
glissading

cutting   cutting steps
crossing a very steep slope
direct very steep ascent/
    descent

Support Position

To attain the support position, hold the axe by its head so that the shaft points vertically downwards. The palm rests on the top of the head while the thumb and first finger curl around the neck of the adze (or as best they can when wearing bulky mitts). The other fingers grip beneath the pick.

Note that the pick points to the rear while walking so that the axe can be quickly brought into the brake position ready for self-arrest. Some people find it more comfortable (and less threatening in a forward stumble) to rotate the head so that the pick points forward, hoping to have the presence of mind to make the reverse switch before applying a self-arrest.

When crossing a relatively gentle slope, simply poke the spike into the ground as you would a walking stick. When more security is required, thrust the shaft deep into the snow. In hard snow set at steeper angles the

Fig 87   *Step kicking in direct ascent. The axe is in the support position.*

shaft may not penetrate to a sufficient depth. In this case it may be better to reverse your grip and embed the pick, allowing the shaft simply to lie against the slope.

Brake Position

In this position the axe is held in a state of greater readiness. The head is gripped as before, but now the other hand grips the lower part of the shaft (which is aligned diagonally across the chest). From this position the pick may be jabbed into steep snow at shoulder level – a particularly useful technique when confronted by a sudden steepening. The great advantage of

Fig 88   Step kicking in descent. Raising
the toe sharpens the heel profile.
The axe is in the support position.

using the axe in this brake position on steep ground is that the self-arrest can be applied very quickly if you slip.

Cutting Position

As the name implies, this is the position to adopt when forced to cut steps. The shaft is held in either hand at a point close to the spike, thereby allowing a full swing with the adze. You may be able to grip the shaft with both hands when cutting from a stable position.

The cutting position is also used when negotiating short but very steep obstacles. In this case, rotate your grip on the shaft so

the pick points forward and can be swung into the slope above your head. The technique is more easily applied during ascent than descent (when the pick is implanted, with some difficulty, at shoulder level). In both cases, one hand grips the shaft while the other seeks additional support from protruding rocks or handholds you have cut in the ice.

ZIGZAGGING ASCENT/ DESCENT *(Figs 89 to 92)*

Whether step kicking or otherwise, steep snow slopes are less tiring when ascended in a series of zigzags. Added support and security comes from the axe, which throughout is held in the support position by the 'uphill' hand.

A standardised, rhythmic approach to zigzagging leads to safer and less tedious ascents of long slopes. In hard snow there is a temptation to take three or four steps before moving the axe to its new position, but this severely upsets balance. Instead it is better to move the axe after every two steps, and to do this while most of your weight is supported by the outside (lower) foot. This procedure applies equally well during descent.

If the slope is steep, or if step security is poor for some other reason, it will be essential to thrust the axe shaft deep into the snow at each placement. During a prolonged ascent this will prove very tiring, but do try to remember that the axe shaft will be your only means of support if the snow suddenly collapses beneath your feet.

An awkward transfer of the axe takes place at the completion of each diagonal (for maximum security it is always held in the uphill hand). Minimise your vulner-

Axe Changeover During Zigzag Ascent

Fig 89   *Hold the axe by the 'uphill' hand in the support position.*

Fig 90   *Face the slope at the end of the diagonal, thrust the axe shaft deep into the snow, and kick an extra large step.*

Fig 91   *Swivel the axe head and transfer hand position (and wrist loop if fitted). One or both hands grip the axe head throughout.*

Fig 92   *Complete the inward turn and resume the ascent on the opposite diagonal. The axe is once again in the 'uphill' hand.*

ability at these moments by observing a set procedure for the changeover (*Figs 89 to 92*). Implant the axe shaft fully and then, while holding the head of the axe with both hands, face the slope and kick two good steps. Now swivel the axe head and transfer the hand position (and wrist loop if used) before completing the inward turn ready to begin the opposite diagonal. Note that the axe shaft remains deeply embedded throughout and that its head is always gripped by at least one hand. Once again this procedure can be applied equally well during descent.

DIRECT ASCENT/ DESCENT

Zigzagging serves no real purpose on steeper slopes. Instead, whether going up or down, simply face the slope and kick steps with the toe of the boot. A single, swinging kick ought to penetrate the snow to a depth sufficient for supporting at least a third of the length of the boot. If not it may be better to cut steps or fit crampons. The axe, meanwhile, will normally be held in the support position or, if the snow is too hard to accept the shaft, in the variant using the pick for support (but if that is the case then the snow is probably also too hard for step kicking).

Ascents and descents secured by the axe held in the brake and cutting positions are usually confined to snow or ice set at a steeper angle; they are more appropriately described in the context of step cutting and cramponing.

Step Cutting

Widespread use of crampons has totally eclipsed the art of step cutting, and mindful of the hours of labour spent cutting lines of steps up and down icy slopes this is no great loss. Nevertheless, many of the small obstacles encountered while winter walking can be quickly negotiated with the aid of a couple of steps, thus saving the ten minutes or so that would otherwise have been spent fitting and removing crampons.

Since most of the fine art of step cutting was directed towards economy of effort on long ascents, the rudiments may be stated much more briefly. They are:

- Cut from a braced position (i.e. with the weight supported by the outside, lower leg).
- Use the adze whenever possible, reserving the pick for hard ice.
- Cut in-sloping steps for security.
- Cut steps close together to avoid making long, unbalancing strides.
- Cut separate steps for each foot (except during diagonal ascents at average gradients).
- Cut big steps in ascent if you think you may later want to descend the same way.
- Chip a handhold if you need more stability while cutting the next set of steps.

Having assimilated these general principles the best way of developing an effective step cutting technique is to practise various methods on safe ground beforehand. You will soon discover that steps in icy snow are best cut using a series of two or three chips working away from the initial, shallow chip; whereas in softer snow a single slice may adequately locate the edge of the boot during diagonal ascents at lesser angles. Note that having cut the next set of steps, movement up into them is secured by holding the axe in one of the standard positions (such as the brake position when cutting up a steep diagonal).

Walking in Crampons

Bristling crampon points will snag on rocks, lumps of ice, loose clothing – anything and everything – if you let them. Gaiters are essential for restraining laces and flapping legwear. Beware also of long rucksack straps which hang perilously close to the rear points during descents. When walking in crampons it is wise to adopt the waddling style of a duck out of water.

Some walkers, fearing damage to precious equipment, habitually remove crampons prior to crossing sections of icy rock, despite the fact that crampons are then at their most beneficial. Leave them on; provided you refrain from leaping about, damage will be confined to a slight blunting of the spikes.

Crampons *ball-up* in certain snow conditions. This means that snow which accumulates between the spikes will eventually render them ineffective. A sharp rap administered by the axe shaft on the side of each foot will dislodge the snowball and temporarily alleviate the problem. You may need to repeat the treatment every three or four steps. After an hour or two the novelty of hitting your legs with a metal pole starts to fade: that is when the timing goes wrong and you trip yourself up. If the condition persists it might be better to remove crampons and to proceed more predictably, if more slowly, without them.

Ascent/Descent in Crampons

(*Figs 93 to 95*)

Crampons largely obviate the need to kick or cut steps, speeding and securing your

Fig 93 *Descent in crampons. Point the feet downslope and take short steps while holding the axe in the brake position in readiness for self-arrest. Note the difficulty experienced with this long walking axe in covering the spike with the lower hand.*

progress considerably, especially during descent. On gentle slopes you can capitalise on this newly acquired freedom by refraining from implanting the axe spike at each alternate stride as before. Instead simply walk with short strides down the slope while holding the axe in the brake position in readiness for self-arrest should the need arise.

Foot placement on sloping ground is notably different when wearing crampons. The general aim is to perforate the surface

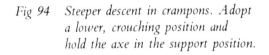

*Fig 94   Steeper descent in crampons. Adopt
            a lower, crouching position and
            hold the axe in the support position.*

*Fig 95   Ascent in crampons. Flex the
            ankles so the maximum
            number of crampon points
            penetrate the surface.*

with as many points as can be comfortably
brought to bear; and that means *flat-footing*
whenever possible. During most descents
and during gentle ascents this presents little
difficulty, but while ascending or crossing
steeper slopes it can place a tremendous
strain on the ankles. Zigzagging eases this to
some extent, as does varying the method of
foot placement.

Stepping-through during zigzag ascents
is practical only at moderate angles. Beyond
those there is too great a risk of snagging the
other foot and tripping over. As the slope
steepens, it is more usual to begin side-
stepping directly up the slope while holding
the axe in either the support or brake

positions. Note that by this method just the
lower boot will happily flat-foot up the
slope; the upper one will tend to edge into
the slope and therefore remain only partially supported. Ankle strain in the lower
leg can be eased by pointing the toes down
the slope.

An alternative technique to side-stepping
on steep slopes is to continue flat-footing
with the lower leg while *front-pointing* with
the upper (this assumes your crampons are
fitted with a set of forward pointing spikes).
The action of implanting the front points is
similar to that used when kicking steps in
direct ascent. Less force is exerted in

111

swinging the foot as compared to normal step kicking, but because only the very front of the boot is supported the technique is cumulatively more tiring on the calf muscles during long ascents.

On very steep ground – such as when negotiating an isolated icy step – it is usual to front-point with both feet while holding the axe in the cutting position. Try to resist the temptation to take large steps, which merely upsets balance and adds to the feeling of insecurity. The pick is embedded in the slope above your head (or at shoulder level during descent) for added support. When using crampons not fitted with front points you will have to kick or cut steps as before.

12 Emergency Techniques for Winter Walking

This chapter looks at some special techniques for use in emergencies. Few of them will ever be used in earnest, but all require practice beforehand if they are to become part of your repertoire of winter skills. Those contemplating ambitious winter outings are strongly advised to attend a course in winter mountaineering (some addresses are given at the back of the book).

SELF-ARREST (*Figs 96 to 105*)

If you stumble from a steep path in summer the result could be a bruised knee; make the same mistake in winter and the consequences could be far worse, perhaps fatal. The self-arrest, or ice-axe brake, offers some hope of halting the slide before it gathers too much momentum, but to have any chance of success it must be applied quickly and correctly.

Skill at self-arrest develops during practice on a safe slope. A 'safe slope' in this context is one which is concave with a gentle run-out, and which is free of icy patches, scree, protruding rocks or any other painful impediment.

For all variants of self-arrest, hold the axe in the brake position. It is important for the lower hand to grip the axe shaft near its end to prevent the spike from jabbing into the snow. This low hand position is difficult to achieve when using a long walking axe. Remember that unless the axe is held very

firmly the braking force exerted through the embedded pick will snatch it from your grasp. With the axe in the brake position, the arrest is completed in two more stages: alignment of the body and application of the brake.

Before applying the brake in head-first slides you must control your body so that you are sliding feet first. To achieve this – whether sliding face up or face down –

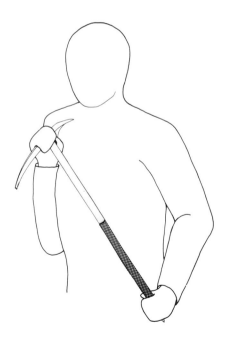

Fig 96   Holding the axe in the 'brake' position during self-arrest.

Self-arrest from a Feet First Slide

Fig 97   Axe in the brake position.

Fig 98   Beginning the sideways roll to apply the brake.

Fig 99   Sideways roll almost completed (lowering the left shoulder and arching the back increases braking effect). Note the axe head tucked close to the shoulder and spike raised clear of the snow. Feet spread wide assist braking, but cramponed feet are raised to avoid initiating a tumbling fall.

Self-arrest from a Head First, Face Down Slide

Fig 100   *Axe in the brake position.*
       The pick is generally applied
       to one side to initiate pivoting
       action.

Fig 101   *Rotation in progress. Note the*
       legs spread wide for stability.

Fig 102   *Sideways rotation complete.*
       The pick has been raised so
       the axe head can be tucked
       close to the shoulder before
       applying the full brake.

Self-arrest from a Head First, Face Up Slide

Fig 103   *Axe in the brake position. The pick is gradually applied to one side to initiate rotation.*

Fig 104   *Rotation in progress.*

Fig 105   *Sideways rotation complete; starting to apply the full brake.*

Practising Self-Arrest

Ideally, undertake self-arrest practice as part of a formal course of instruction in winter skills. Otherwise, consider following this basic programme.

Precautions
- Choose an ice-free slope which is concave (i.e. becomes shallower as it descends) and which has a long run-out uninterrupted by outcrops, boulders, scree, and so on.
- Wear waterproof trousers and jacket to stay dry, but remember that these will dramatically increase your sliding speed. Begin practising where the slope is gentle.
- Remove crampons, rucksack and anything else (e.g. a scarf) which is likely to get in the way.
- Remove the axe wrist or chest loop and fit the spike bung, or cover it with padding taped in place.

Procedure
- Only one person at a time on the slope.
- Cut a large 'launching pad' from which to begin the slides.
- Reascend to one side of the practice slope to avoid pitting the surface.
- Master each stage before progressing to the next.
- Repeat the practice under different snow conditions (hard snow, wet snow, powder, etc.) and at least once each subsequent winter as a refresher.

Sample Programme

1. Practise holding the axe in correct brake position. On level ground, simulate rolling over to apply brake. Repeat with axe head held in other hand.
2. At the launch pad, lie face down, feet down and with the axe in the brake position. Raise the pick slightly (i.e. release the brake) so you begin to slide. Reapply the break. Repeat several times as you slide down the slope. Reascend and repeat with axe held on other side.
3. With axe in brake position, sit down, lie back and slide down feet first. Roll on to side (remember to roll around the 'braking' shoulder), begin applying brake, and complete roll to attain the full braking position. Repeat with axe held on opposite side.
4. Holding axe in brake position, kneel on launch pad then lie face down with arms stretched forward (in the manner of a crawling soldier with rifle). Hold position using pick implanted to one side. Raise pick to begin slide then gradually reapply causing body to pivot around it. When feet are pointing downslope, raise pick and tuck axe close to shoulder before applying full brake. Repeat on other side.
5. Repeat 4 above, but lying on back with axe initially held across chest.
6. When confident, walk upright across slope with axe in support position and simulate falls – forwards, backwards, sideways. Repeat with axe in other hand.
7. Finally, consider practising while wearing a rucksack and tied to a rope (probably not worth the risk of wearing crampons, but simulate by raising feet as if to avoid cartwheeling). Zigzag up the slope and get your partner to pull you over without warning by tugging on the free end of the rope. Though potentially dangerous, this exercise is true to life and so is worth risking a couple of times.

Don't assume you can now arrest any slide: in reality there will be ice, rocks, powder snow, crampons. In fact, you may never have the chance to show off your expertise. Preventing a slip happening in the first place is the greater skill.

apply the pick to one side (not too enthusiastically) to encourage the body to pivot around it. When the feet are pointing down the slope the full brake can be applied as follows.

When sliding feet down and face up – or, more likely, on your side – the sideways roll into the face down braking position is made around the 'braking' shoulder (i.e. the shoulder at which the axe head is tucked). Rolling in the opposite direction succeeds only in jabbing the spike into the slope, with the risk of having the axe torn from your hands. Having achieved the correct body position, the pick brake is applied progressively but fully by bearing down on it with the shoulder. In soft snow, arching the back intensifies braking. If the pick still slices through without effect, rotate the axe head and try braking with the adze.

A crucial aspect of self-arrest technique is to keep the axe head tight to the braking shoulder throughout by 'locking' the arm which holds it. The other hand pulls up on the spike to increase pick pressure and to minimise the risk of the spike diving into the snow. Splayed boots assist braking, but try to raise cramponed feet from hard snow to prevent cartwheeling.

Self-arrest is by no means a foolproof technique. Caught off guard and hindered by rucksack and crampons, your slide may develop into an uncontrollable fall before you can even begin to apply the brake. Moreover, the brake will be ineffective in powder snow, on ice, or on thin snow overlying rock. Ironically the snow conditions most favourable to successful self-arrest exist when a slip is least likely to occur.

GLISSADING

Glissading is a technique used for the rapid and sometimes controlled descent of a known safe slope (i.e. concave, gentle run-out, with no drops, rocks or icy patches). It is an exciting pastime fraught with danger – not least from a flailing ice-axe if you lose control. There have been many serious accidents. You should never feel obliged to glissade just because others seem to think it is safe – it rarely is.

Theory describes glissades in both standing and squatting postures, whereas in fact you may as well begin as you will certainly finish – sitting down. The technique is simple: sit upright in the snow, legs slightly apart (no crampons), and slide down like a human toboggan. Loud whooping noises are optional! The axe, meanwhile, is held across the chest in the brake position. If you want to slow down, press the spike of the axe in the snow to one side. If you want to stop, roll over in the appropriate direction and self-arrest using the ice-axe brake. If you want to remain dry with nerves and body intact, get to your feet and walk down.

ROPE PROTECTION
(Figs 106 & 107)

The principles of rope protection are the same winter or summer; Chapter 8 describes the essentials. The main practical difference is that anchors will be much more difficult to locate under a covering of snow. Nevertheless, when faced by small rock steps on a ridge or gully (typical situations when rope protection might be desirable) it should be possible to excavate a rock spike or chockstone. Some obstacles, such as ice bulges, frozen stream courses, and cornices, are not so accommodating; forced into a direct confrontation you might find yourself reluctantly anchoring directly to the snow or ice.

Anchors in snow or ice are comparatively weak and unreliable. Thankfully a fall in these circumstances is more likely to result in a fast slide than a dramatic aerial. By digging in (sitting back with legs apart and braced in snow troughs) it ought to be

possible to arrest the fall without any of its force being transferred to the anchor.

Assuming no specialised snow and ice equipment is available, the most useful anchor in snow will be the horizontally buried ice-axe (refer to *Fig 106* for method). For this to be at all effective, however, the snow must be of firm composition and adequate depth.

Cutting the T-slot for a buried axe anchor takes time. Occasionally it may be

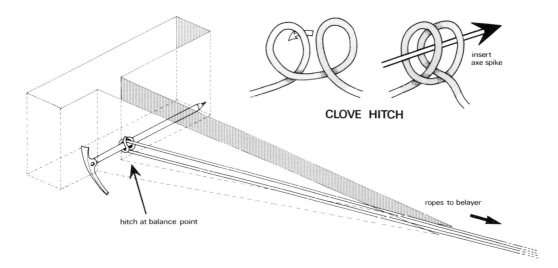

CLOVE HITCH

insert
axe spike

ropes to belayer

hitch at balance point

Fig 106   *Anchoring in snow: a horizontally buried ice-axe. Cut a deep T-shaped slot in the snow; the actual depth depends on snow consistency. The upright of the T points downslope, i.e. in the likely direction of rope pull during a fall. Form a clove hitch in the anchor sling (or main rope) and position at the balance point of the axe shaft. The hitch will be more secure if the cross-over part of the knot is positioned on the uphill side as shown. Press the axe into the base of the slot as shown. Check that the anchor sling/rope lies deep in its slot and in a straight line. Stamp leg troughs in the snow about 3m downslope from the buried axe and secure yourself to the anchor sling/rope. A waist belay from a sitting position will put minimum strain on the anchor.*

119

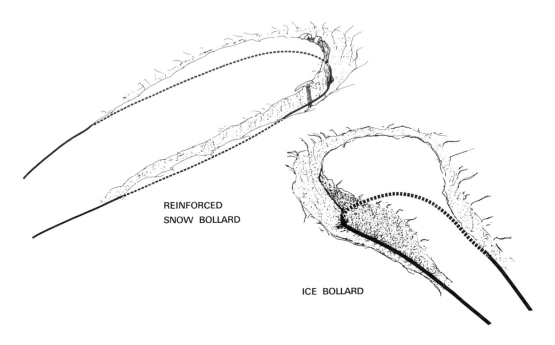

Fig 107   Bollard anchors in snow and ice.

acceptable to anchor to an axe thrust like a stake into hard snow, for instance when steadying a companion who is cutting steps down a short incline, but be under no illusions as to what loads such an anchor is able to withstand. It may do no more than prevent the belayer from inadvertently slithering off the ledge while paying out rope. When using this type of anchor you must expect to take the full force of the fall yourself.

Ice-axe anchors in soft snow are wholly unreliable. An alternative in these conditions might be to cut a snow bollard. This is just what it sounds like: a large diameter (two metres or more), elongated mushroom around which the anchor rope is looped. A slot depth of about 50cm at the sides and rear prevents the loop from riding up or skimming off the top snow layer. Belay from a ledge stamped a few metres down-slope to avoid disturbing its structure.

Despite these precautions the anchor loop still wants to slice through the snow like a cheese wire. Reinforcement of the bollard with ice-axe and rucksack should stop that happening.

The equivalent bollard on ice need not be so massive (perhaps 50cm across the short axis and 15cm in depth), but it would require a more pronounced lip at the rear to prevent the anchor loop from lifting off. Ice often forms in layers, so don't be surprised if your cutting shatters the top couple of centimetres. If it does shatter you have no option but to choose another site and begin again.

MOVING TOGETHER *(Fig 108)*

Occasionally you will want to stay roped while walking across easy but exposed terrain, such as along a narrow ridge. In this case, shorten the length of rope between you and your companion to about eight metres, coil the excess around your shoulder and tie it off at the waist using a figure-of-eight knot, otherwise the coil becomes a noose! Finally, take up a couple of small hand coils to be let out or taken in as necessary.

A nagging worry while moving together is that if one person falls the other will also be dragged off – a fear not without foundation both in logic and in history (remembering the fate of Whymper's party on the Matterhorn). Things are not completely hopeless, however. When ridge traversing, for instance, the rope stretched between you may be flicked over and around natural spikes as you move along, affording at least some basic security. As a last resort, a quick-witted second will wait to see which side of the ridge the leader falls and then nimbly step over the opposite side to act as a counterbalance. A foolproof plan has yet to be devised to protect the party from an unimaginative second who insists on falling unannounced behind the leader's back!

Opportunities for mobile anchors are few when moving together on a snow slope. One useful method of belaying the rope 'on the move' – the New Zealand ice-axe foot brake – generates friction around the axe shaft and boot. However, in view of the terrain most likely to be encountered while walking, and of the variability of British snow conditions, a more realistic contingency plan is simply to drop your hand coils and throw yourself on to the snow in the self-arrest position. Assuming your companion does the same, hopefully one or other of your braking attempts will prove successful.

Fig 108 Moving together along a snow crest (Aonach Beag). Leader and second are on opposite sides of the ridge (note the hand coils).

Moving together is a valuable technique when route finding under conditions of poor visibility, not least because of the very real possibility of walking on to a cornice or over the edge of a cliff at night or during a white-out. For obvious reasons it is wise to arrange yourselves so that the rope lies at right angles to the suspected cornice or cliff top. This means that when navigating along the rim of plateau (a typical application) you will walk along parallel lines with the rope stretched between you. Once again, both of you need to be ready to drop instantly into the self-arrest position.

121

NEGOTIATING CORNICES
(Fig 109)

Cornices typically form along ridge crests, at the rims of corries, and at the upper exits of gullies. All are potentially unstable and liable to collapse without warning. They are best avoided if at all possible, although it can happen that you are faced with no alternative but to find a way through. If you find yourself confronting these and other serious obstacles on a regular basis then you are winter *climbing*, not *walking*, and would do well to acquire the appropriate equipment and knowledge.

Cornices in Scotland can develop to such massive proportions that a direct assault is quite out of the question, but you would be unlucky not to find a flanking route where the bulge is less pronounced. Even so, the exit may steepen disconcertingly during the final few metres. Security will be improved by kicking big steps and by driving in the axe shaft fully at each upward move. You should consider using rope protection, depending on the likely consequences of a fall, but bear in mind that the snow immediately beneath a cornice is unlikely to have an ideal consistency for anchoring.

The cornice may curl and overhang even at its shallowest. In this case there is no option but to cut back the lip using the axe and a great deal of energy. Hopefully it will be enough to lessen the angle by forming a slot, although in extreme cases – and this really must be an act of desperation – you may be forced to tunnel through. Before committing yourself to a lot of unnecessary hard work, however, suspect a previous ascent and look for an old slot or tunnel which might have since drifted over: clearing a ready-made exit would be much easier than starting afresh.

Fig 109 *Glyder Fawr. When cornices collapse the break line extends some distance into the plateau or ridge which supports them. It is very important to keep well back from the edge.*

Descent ov~r a previously unbreached corniced rim is a thoroughly intimidating experience. First prepare an elaborate anchor on the plateau, well back from the suspected cornice break line, and rope up. The leader, belayed by the second, now descends with rope protection from above, cutting a deep slot and furnishing it with large steps for the benefit of the second. Once below the barrier, the leader moves to one side before anchoring (probably to a buried axe). Communication may be difficult, especially if a wind is blowing, so a pre-arranged set of rope tugs could inform the second that it is time to follow.

DIGGING A SNOW CAVE
(*Figs 110 & 111*)

A snow cave can give valuable emergency shelter if you are forced to bivouac. Unfortunately its excavation will demand a great deal of time and effort. In almost every circumstance it would be better to save that time and energy and to persevere with the descent. A decision to stop and dig in will not have been taken lightly. Nevertheless, the occasion may one day arise – perhaps when someone in your party is injured or suffering from hypothermia – when you are faced with absolutely no alternative. With that in mind it is worth digging a snow cave on an off-day, if only to get some idea of the scale of the undertaking.

Snow of a suitable depth and consistency is the first prerequisite. There is little chance of satisfying either condition on an open slope, so look for snow drifts which may have formed in the lee of boulders, stone walls, stream banks, or other natural features. In desperation you may even risk tunnelling into the base of a stable-looking cornice.

Making caves is wet and sweaty work, so you will want to remove warm clothes (but retain waterproofs) in order to keep them dry for the night. Under ideal practice conditions a fit person can dig a rudimentary cave for two and be resident within the hour. In a genuine emergency – when the weather is likely to be poor, the snow imperfect, and your strength already failing – a more realistic minimum would be twice that or more.

Fig 110   *An emergency snow cave.*
Digging horizontally into a
drift saves time and energy.

Having found a suitable site, the next job is to mine a slot directly into the drift. Eventually the slot will become a narrow tunnel entrance, but at this stage it is more important to have adequate digging space. Then excavate cavities at either side of the slot to form the main chamber. If two people are digging they will cut slots a body length apart and excavate single cavities towards each other, meeting in the middle. One of the slots will then be completely sealed off.

Snow shovels and saws make quick work of excavation, but there is little point in practising with tools you are unlikely to have with you under genuine circumstances.

Fig 111   On the inside looking out.

That means you will be reduced to using an ice-axe, and the long-shafted walking variety are very unwieldy indeed. For economy of effort, try mining the cavities in blocks rather than by scraping. This is easiest to do if the face is first sliced into a lattice using the pick, later chipping out the blocks with the adze.

Having completed the chamber, the next task is partially to close the entry in order to form a crawl tunnel; excavated blocks will come in useful here for re-roofing the original slot. Ideally the tunnel entrance will now be at a lower level than the chamber, preventing warm air generated within from escaping too readily. A rucksack adequately seals the entrance once everyone is inside, while a hole poked through the roof supplements ventilation. Overnight drifting will bury equipment left outside, so everything should be brought into the chamber; besides which you will want an axe inside in order to maintain the vents and perhaps to dig yourself out in the morning. An exception is the axe planted in the roof as a search aid to rescuers.

Permanent emergency shelters serve a few of the more popular mountains. These

Fig 112   *The Ben Nevis summit shelter stands high on its plinth during lean winters.*

Fig 113   *The Ben Nevis summit shelter one year later. The snow is much deeper and in this near white-out only the door frame can be seen.*

erections vary from tomb-like metal boxes to substantial stone-built sheds. Locations are normally marked on maps, but it would be unwise to abandon all other evacuation plans in the hope of finding one. In con-ditions of poor visibility and severe drifting you might pass within metres of the shelter without ever knowing of its existence.

SOME SPECIAL TOPICS

Fig 114   Moel Siabod – the east ridge above Llyn y Foel.

13 Mountain Weather

This chapter expands on some important aspects of meteorology which have been mentioned but not detailed in previous chapters.

CHARACTERISTIC AIRSTREAMS *(Fig 115)*

We have seen already that snow conditions depend on the prevailing winter weather regime – freeze/thaw, mild or cold. Those regimes have parallels in summer and, under the more general titles of polar maritime, tropical maritime and polar continental, represent the three most common characteristic airstreams to influence British weather.

Polar Maritime

This airstream is responsible for the usual cold and showery mix of British weather. Typically, a train of low pressure systems (called *lows* or *depressions*) will track eastwards across northern Britain, drawing cold and moisture-laden air down from polar regions of the north-west. Blustery showers are symptomatic, and our mountain regions – being so exposed to the westerly winds – will attract the worst of them. From late autumn through to spring these showers may fall as hail or snow. Sunny periods often separate the outbreaks of rain, giving varied and invigorating weather.

Tropical Maritime

Warm air will be drawn up from the more tropical regions of the Atlantic when the train of lows traverses further south. The airstream is moisture laden, though much less erratic in behaviour than the polar maritime. Under its influence the mountains of the west may be cloaked in mist for several days at a time and subject to periodic bouts of rain or drizzle.

Polar Continental

This dry, easterly wind sweeps across from Siberia, usually as a consequence of a high pressure system centred to the north of Britain. In summer it brings warm and dry

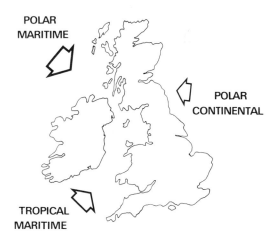

Fig 115   *Airstreams which commonly influence British weather.*

weather, perhaps lasting for many days. In winter the wind is bitterly cold and temperatures in the mountains may remain at or below freezing for days or even weeks at a time.

PRESSURE

Distributions

Weather maps show the distribution of high and low air pressure over and around Britain. This pressure topography is shaped from *isobars* (lines which connect points of equal pressure) in a similar manner to the contour lines of a geographical map. In this case, however, the topography is forever changing as air masses constantly shift in an attempt to equalise pressure anomalies.

These winds are subject to a global phenomenon (described in physics by laws governing movement across rotating spheres) whereby they circulate around pressure peaks and hollows: anticlockwise around lows and clockwise around highs. This retards the filling and levelling of the pressure topography, which explains why weather conforms to some sort of predictable pattern.

Systems

Highs

Unfortunately these stable and persistent features are reluctant to form over Britain. Light winds and clear skies are typical, giving warm days and cool nights (but cold throughout in winter). Less resilient high

Fig 115   A cloud sea spills into the Ogwen Valley.

pressure features, known as *ridges*, may intervene between successive areas of low pressure, granting a brief respite from bad weather.

Lows

These mobile and unstable features are associated with bad weather. Fortunately they fill relatively quickly (within a few days), so prolonged bad weather is unusual. Irregularities in a low pressure system are known as *fronts*. The passage of these fronts is accompanied by a more or less predictable weather cycle which begins with clear skies, deteriorates into a band of steady rain, and ends with a period of sunshine and showers – and all in the space of 24 hours or so. Weak low pressure features known as *troughs* may ripple through an established high pressure system, bringing a few hours of poor weather.

PASSAGE OF FRONTS
(Figs 117 & 118)

The passage of a frontal system will trigger a series of rapid changes in the weather, affecting temperature, precipitation and visibility. Prediction of these changes is of great importance to the hill walker since the progress of a front will raise or dash hopes for a fine tomorrow. Meteorologists plot that progress using isobaric charts drawn up from pressure measurements. Insensitive to these fluctuations, the hill walker will monitor instead the approach of characteristic cloud patterns.

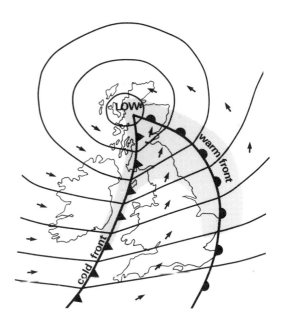

Fig 117 A typical weather chart during unsettled weather. The shaded area indicates rain belt, the arrows indicate surface wind direction.

Influence of Mountains

Mountains disrupt the smooth passage of weather systems, intensifying their worst aspects in the process. Weather in the mountains is consequently colder, wetter and windier than in the surrounding lowlands.

Temperature

Atmospheric pressure decreases with altitude; air rising over a mountain barrier expands according to this reduction in pressure and so loses heat. This rate of cooling can be calculated according to the *adiabatic lapse rate*, which varies from about 1°C per 100m in dry air to about 1°C per 200m in very humid air. Lapse rates explain

129

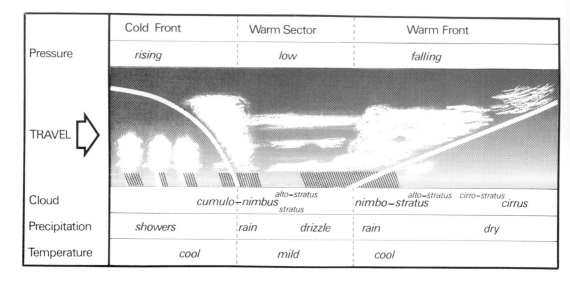

	Cold Front	Warm Sector	Warm Front
Pressure	rising	low	falling
	TRAVEL ⇨		
Cloud	cumulo–nimbus	alto–stratus / stratus	nimbo–stratus / alto–stratus cirro–stratus cirrus
Precipitation	showers	rain drizzle	rain dry
Temperature	cool	mild	cool

Fig 118   *The passage of a frontal system. The procession of cloud types heralds the arrival and passage of warm and cold fronts.*

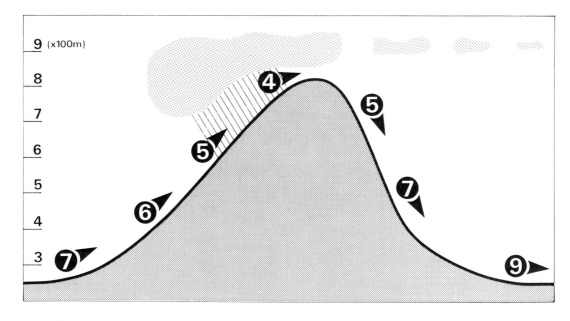

Fig 119   *Adiabatic cooling. Mountain tops typically suffer lower temperatures and higher levels of rainfall.*

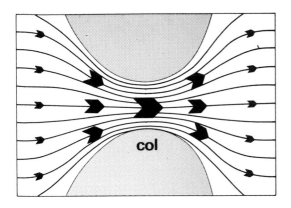 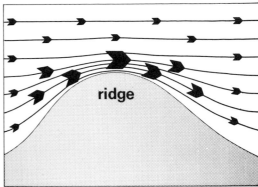

Fig 120   Winds funnel through cols and over ridge crests at dramatically increased speeds.

the great variation in temperatures experienced between valley and summit.

Precipitation (Fig 119)

Adiabatic cooling also influences the level of precipitation. Cooled air is less able to sustain its vapour content, so when moist air rises and cools some of its vapour condenses into clouds. The clouds re-evaporate once the air begins to descend (and to warm) on the far side of the barrier. This explains the phenomenon of stationary clouds seen hovering over mountain tops in apparent defiance of a strong wind. If the moisture content and degree of cooling is sufficient rain will fall on the windward side of the barrier.

Wind (Fig 120)

Mountains project into the airstream like boulders in a river; intense local concentrations of wind at ridge crests and between cols contrast with the eerie calm of lee slopes and sheltered valleys.

131

14 Mountain Navigation

Previous chapters have dealt with the fundamentals of map reading and route finding; accordingly, this one will try to confine itself to a summary of techniques essential to navigation in difficult conditions.

THE COMPASS (Figs 121 & 122)

A compass functions on the principle that a finely balanced and slender magnet will align itself to the earth's magnetic field. In other words, the red-tipped needle points north. Elegantly simple! Arranged in a circle around the needle pivot are the *points* of the compass: north, east, south and west.

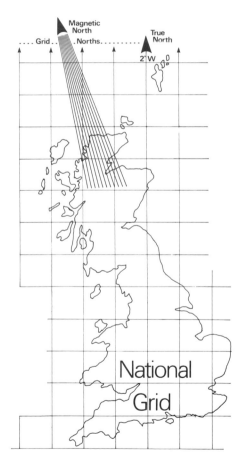

Fig 122 Note that since grid north is not a unique point, the magnetic deviation depends on your position as well as the present location of magnetic north.

Fig 121 A type 4 Silva compass.

132

The compass housing marks those four main points and also the 360 degrees of a circle, starting at north with 0 and increasing clockwise. Using these degree increments your direction of travel – your *bearing* – is referred to as being angled 'x degrees from north'. But which north? There are three: *true*, *magnetic* and *grid*.

Map grid lines are aligned with grid north; while the compass needle is aligned to magnetic north. True north may be ignored. Magnetic north deviates from grid north by a few degrees, the precise amount depending on your position and on the location of the shifting magnetic north pole (which at present lies somewhere beneath northern Canada). In Britain during the mid-1980s that magnetic variation amounted to about five degrees west of grid north. Ordnance Survey maps indicate the variation whenever bearings are transferred from map to compass (added) or vice versa (subtracted). A simple mnemonic reminds us which is which: *grid to mag. add*.

Setting the Map

This simple procedure was fully described in Chapter 5, but will be summarised here for completeness.

To align the map with the terrain, place the compass flat on the map surface and rotate both together until the compass needle lies parallel with the map grid lines (i.e. red north needle points towards the 'top' of the map). The magnetic variation may be ignored in this exercise. In good weather, with distinctive landmarks visible, it ought now to be possible to confirm your position.

Backbearing *(Fig 123)*

Occasionally you may not be able to confirm your position simply by setting the map and referring to landmarks. Perhaps you are following a ridge crest among rolling hills; you know where you are in one dimension (along the ridge), but not in the other (distance travelled along the ridge). The answer is to take the bearing of some feature to one side – it could be a farm or small lake – and then transfer the line of the bearing to the map. The cross where that line intersects the ridge gives your position. The following details this procedure:

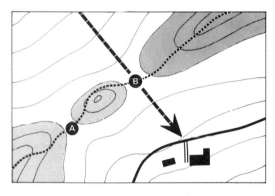

Fig 123   A backbearing on the farm buildings confirms your position at B, not A.

1.   Aim the 'direction of travel' arrow on the compass baseplate towards the landmark.
2.   Rotate the compass housing until its north mark coincides with the north (red) needle.
3.   Note the magnetic bearing given by the index mark which shows through the housing (it is in the same line as the baseplate arrow).
4.   Subtract the magnetic variation at the index mark by rotating the housing the

required number of degrees.

5.   Place the compass on the map (there is no need to worry about keeping the map set) so that the housing north mark points towards grid north.

6.   Keeping the compass in correct alignment, move the baseplate until its side edge touches the identified landmark.

7.   Confirm your position by noting where this edge, or its continuation, crosses your ridge (stream, track, or whatever).

The intersection of one or two other back-bearings would give further confirmation of your position, but if you can identify that many landmarks you probably know where you are anyway.

Aspect of a Slope *(Fig 124)*

It can be extremely difficult to confirm position while contouring a featureless slope in mist. The following method offers some hope:

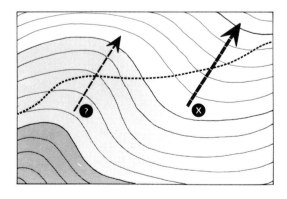

Fig 124   A bearing taken directly down-slope puts your position at X. But beware the similarity of contour line curvature which could place you at '?'.

1.   Aim the baseplate arrow directly down the slope.

2.   Rotate the housing to obtain the bearing.

3.   Subtract the magnetic variation.

4.   Place the compass on the map so that the housing north mark points towards grid north.

5.   While maintaining its correct orientation, slide the baseplate across your approximate position until its edge cuts across the contour lines at right angles (i.e. pointing directly down the slope).

6.   Your position on the slope should be somewhere along the line of that edge.

Walking on a Bearing
(Figs 125 to 128)

So far the compass has been used only to confirm your present position, but in order to proceed you need a direction to follow. Obtained from the map and transferred to the compass, that bearing will keep you on course as you walk towards your destination.

1.   Join up your present and intended positions on the map using the baseplate edge; i.e. the direction of travel indicated by the baseplate arrow (there is no need to set the map).

2.   Rotate the housing until its north mark points towards grid north.

3.   Read off the grid bearing at the index mark.

4.   Add the magnetic variation by rotating the housing the appropriate number of degrees (remember: 'grid to mag, add').

5.   Hold the compass level and in front of you (well away from ice-axes or other metal objects) and then rotate yourself and the compass until the red needle points to the north mark on the compass housing.

Fig 125   Obtain the required bearing from the map.

Fig 126   Add the magnetic variation.

Fig 127   *Align the north needle with the north mark on the housing, then follow the direction indicated by the baseplate arrow.*

6. The baseplate 'direction of travel' arrow now indicates the whereabouts of your destination.

Timing and Pacing (Fig 129)

A compass bearing has only one dimension. Nevertheless, provided you are able to follow that bearing without deviation you can be certain of arriving at your destination. But when? The question has more than academic interest. Walking on a bearing is never error free. Suppose, for instance, your accuracy lies within a ten degree angle (five degrees either side of the actual bearing). After travelling a few hundred metres the arc of possible error is now many metres across; it may even exceed the limit of visibility. In the mist you could have passed beyond your target – perhaps a summit cairn or shelter – without ever being aware of its presence. Timing or pacing adds an essential extra dimension to the bearing, that of length.

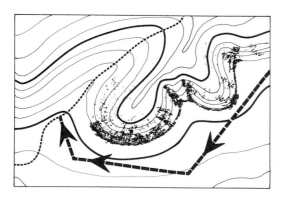

Fig 128   *Combine a sequence of bearings with timing or pacing to avoid obstacles.*

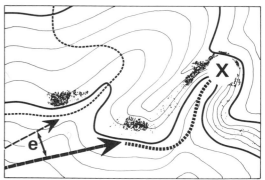

Fig 129   *Small errors, inevitable when following a bearing, could lead you into a false feature and unexpected difficulties at X. Timing or pacing the leg makes this mistake much less likely.*

A simple formula for estimating time is based on Naismith's Rule: allow twelve minutes for each kilometre travelled, plus one minute for each ten-metre contour crossed in ascent. The rule assumes average conditions, taking no account of heavy loads, wind, awkward terrain, and so on. Variations to Naismith's Rule take some of those factors into account, but for most purposes it is enough to make rule of thumb allowances as you go along.

Under more difficult conditions – at night or during a white-out in winter – time estimates by themselves lack precision. Instead it is better to measure the distance travelled along a bearing by counting paces. The method works best over relatively level ground, and is especially useful when attempting to find a point somewhere on a mist-shrouded plateau. Ideally you should calculate your average pace length before-hand (by pacing out a measured distance) and then make adjustments to it for awkward terrain encountered on the actual leg (pace length in crusty snow, for instance, will be very much less than over short grass). As a very rough guide, a hundred metres of typical (but level) hill terrain is equivalent to about 150 paces.

LOCATING A POINT

Armed with a compass bearing and an estimate of time or paces, you should – in theory – now be in a position to stride off confidently into the gloom. Unfortunately things are never so simple. Even quite small errors compound themselves, so that at the end of a murky leg you may discover only more murk. Sometimes it is better to assume that errors will be made and to choose destinations accordingly.

Attack Point *(Fig 130)*

When navigating in bad weather it is essential to know where you are at all times. That means covering short legs (ideally 500m or less) between easily identified points, even though this may involve approaching your goal in a series of dog-legs. An attack point is simply a distinctive landmark near to your actual but indistinct destination. It could be a pronounced col, gully exit, lake, or other easily identified feature. Having first located the attack point it will be easier to navigate the short distance between it and your ill-defined summit, descent ridge, or whatever.

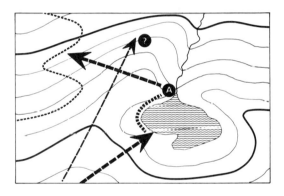

Fig 130   A small error in a direct bearing could lead to uncertainty. A slightly longer but more certain 'dog-leg' approach uses the lake as an intermediate goal.

Aiming-off *(Fig 131)*

When aiming towards a junction situated somewhere along an extended feature such as a ridge crest or stream (it may be a subsidiary ridge or tributary you want to locate and follow), you risk arriving at the feature without being certain if the junction

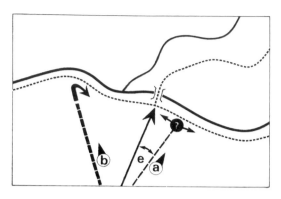

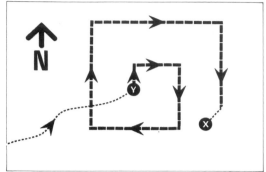

Fig 131   A small error in the direct bearing 'a' leads to uncertainty: which way to turn to find the bridge, left or right? By deliberately aiming-off on bearing 'b' you will know to turn right on reaching the stream.

Fig 132   Destination expected to be at Y and eventually located at X after conducting a spiral search.

lies to the left or right. A more reliable approach is deliberately to aim-off by a hundred metres or so. This way you can be certain of knowing which way to turn in order to locate the junction.

Searching for a Point *(Fig 132)*

However much care is taken with bearings and paces, and despite making full use of attack points and aiming-off, you may arrive at your supposed destination to find no indication whatsoever of its presence. With two or three people in the party it may be enough to spread out laterally when approaching the probable site, thereby increasing the likelihood of it being seen. If this fails, or if you are alone, the only sure way of locating the point is to begin a spiral search.

Guided by the compass, walk north for a distance equal to the limit of visibility (suppose this is ten metres); now turn east and walk twenty paces; south and walk thirty paces; west forty paces; north fifty paces; east sixty. In other words, expand the spiral at each leg by a distance equivalent to the limit of visibility. The spiral continues to grow until such time as you locate the point – or collapse in dizzy despair!

Special Precautions

By definition the conditions under which you will be forced to rely on accurate navigation will be difficult and demoralising. It can be of great help, therefore, to prepare essential bearings the previous evening; perhaps those to the summit from the end of an approach ridge, or from the summit to the start of a steep descent.

In a winter white-out it may be necessary to rope up while navigating along a ridge or the edge of a plateau, the danger of walking over a cliff or cornice in these conditions being a very real one. Obviously the party walks so that the rope is strung out at right angles to the edge.

When walking on a bearing you will find yourself constantly seeking out small features ahead, such as boulders or cairns, which happen to coincide with your line of travel. So instead of being preoccupied with each shiver of the compass needle you are now able to walk confidently from one feature to the next while maintaining a greater level of accuracy. However, winter snow cover obscures most of these intermediate landmarks, magnifying the potential error. One solution is to send someone ahead – a mobile landmark – to walk along the line of the bearing, corrected by your shouts each time they deviate to left or right. When greater accuracy is required, your companion should wait while you approach counting paces, the manoeuvre being repeated until you arrive at your destination.

15 Mountain Emergencies

Several comprehensive texts have been written about these topics. They instruct the group leader and rescue team member, but the average hill walker will recoil from them in confusion. With that in mind these notes will describe only what action can be reasonably expected of a non-specialist suddenly confronted by an emergency (the bibliography suggests further reading).

FIRST AID

Minor Ailments

Grouped under this heading are complaints which, at least in the British hills, may be considered minor or rarely serious. The threat here is not so much to life and limb as to the continuing enjoyment of the walk and remaining days of the holiday.

Blisters

Blisters and rubbed heels have affected each and every one of us at some time; those claiming otherwise have short memories. Nevertheless, preventative measures reduce the risk tenfold, and well-fitting, broken-in boots and socks are a good start. Remember to retighten laces at intervals during the walk as boots and socks gradually bed down.

The trick with blisters is to catch them before they can get a foothold, as it were, by covering the affected area with a suitable dressing. Ordinary sticking plaster is conspicuously ineffective in preventing growth in blisters, which explains the recent proliferation of commercial blister remedies. So many of these have found their way on to the shelves of sports shops and chemists that the dilemma for regular sufferers is today one of selection.

Large blisters may be popped using a pin which has been sterilised over a flame. Complete the treatment by taping a sterile dressing over the affected area. Minimise further abrasion by padding the area with a bandage or extra sock.

Basic First-aid Kit

Basic first-aid kits may be bought ready-packed or compiled individually and packed in a plastic lunch box. No one will entirely agree on the contents; the following is merely a suggested package:

Small individual plasters
Roll of zinc oxide plaster
Crêpe bandage
Triangular bandages (2)
Large wound dressings (2)
Blister dressings
Aspirins
Scissors
Nappy pin
Pencil and paper

Extras in summer:

Sun cream
Insect repellent
Salt tablets

140

Fig 133   The recovery position.

Sunburn

Hill walkers are more vulnerable than most to sunburn (or else more careless). Dry winds prime the skin, which is then exposed to the sun for many hours at a time – often including the midday period and with minimal rotation. Exposure at altitude is more damaging, not only because of snow reflections but from the greater intensity of ultraviolet light. Special precautions are always taken in Alpine areas (nose guards, glacier cream, and so on), whereas at the more modest 1,000m altitudes of British hills even basic protection offered by sun cream, long-sleeved shirts and lightweight trousers is commonly renounced. The penance is to suffer the rolling and grinding of heavy rucksack straps on red-raw shoulders. Astute retailers rack 'afterburn' lotions next to their blister kits!

Mild Heat Exhaustion

Liquid losses while hill walking are considerable at any time of year. Dry summer days merely aggravate the situation by depriving the ridge walker of the means to replenish them. Prevention is simply to arrange for a steady intake of liquid during the day by making repeated stops at streams and/or using a water bottle. An early start ensures that the hard uphill walking will be completed in the cool of the morning.

The condition can be identified by some or all of the following symptoms: cramp, thirst, faintness and tiredness. If the condition develops despite precautions shade the victim from sunlight, remove unnecessary clothing, and encourage him to drink liquid in sips. Salt tablets may also be given (as directed). When sufficiently recovered the victim should be able to cope with an unhurried descent. It would be most unwise to resume the ascent, however, even if recovery is dramatic.

Snow Blindness

Precautions against snow blindness are taken as a matter of course in the Alps and other high altitude regions, but not within the less dazzling world of British winter mountaineering. Nevertheless, a bright spring day over snow-covered hills could strain unprotected eyes to the point of

First-aid Checklist

Approach
No heroics – consider the safety of others and yourself. Calm and reassure the casualty (and yourself) and stress that rescuers are coming.

Check Breathing
Clear airway if necessary using a hooked finger to remove obstructions (vomit, blood, and so on). Turn casualty to lie on left side in recovery position (*Fig 133*) unless you suspect spinal injury. This helps maintain a clear airway.

Check for Severe Bleeding
Apply direct pressure from a pad to stop bleeding. Elevate the limb.

Check for Broken Bones
Don't move the casualty if spinal injury is suspected. Immobilise other fractures using improvised splints and slings.

Monitor Condition
Keep casualty warm and comfortable while awaiting rescue; protect from wind and insulate from ground. Reassure casualty and monitor condition regularly.

discomfort. Goggles or hooded glasses are usual at high altitudes, whereas ordinary sunglasses will suffice in Britain (although goggles offer better protection from wind-driven hail). If the condition develops in someone who has not taken these precautions there is nothing you can do while on the mountain other than improvise eye shading to stop it getting worse.

Mild Frost-bite

In a British winter it is usually the debilitating effect of cold – not frost-bite – which is of greater concern. Even so, the early stages of frost-bite (heralded by local loss of colour and feeling) will strike if for some reason the body's extremities are deprived of their normal degree of insulation, such as through saturated boots or lost hat or gloves. Winter climbers, committed to their sunless gullies for long periods, are generally more sensitive to the danger and take elaborate precautions. Walkers could learn from them by wearing gaiters over carefully treated boot uppers; by fitting wrist security loops to their mitts; and by carrying spare hat, mitts and socks.

If frost-bite is suspected it is wise not to attempt exotic treatments dimly remembered from boys' adventure comics. Rubbing, with snow or anything else, should also be avoided. Moreover, if the victim is also suffering from hypothermia vigorous attempts at improving blood circulation in the extremities will reduce core temperature still further – possibly with fatal consequences. Apart from making ordinary attempts at rewarming a mobile victim (such as placing hands under the armpits and replacing wet socks or mitts with dry spares), your energy and resourcefulness would be better spent escaping the hostile environment which undoubtedly brought on the condition in the first place.

If on reaching the valley feeling has not returned, resist amateur attempts at rewarming with hot water and seek proper medical help.

Hypothermia (exposure)

Mountain hypothermia (lowered body temperature) is preconditioned by a conspiracy of adverse circumstances. These include: inadequate protection from the weather; exhaustion from struggling through deep snow or against the wind; and lack of food. Hypothermia is clearly less of a mishap than the culmination of a sequence of errors. Here is a summary of what action you might take when preventative measures have failed (consult one of the texts listed in the bibliography for a complete description of hypothermia):

- Recognise early signs in your companion – muddled thinking, quietness, stumbling – not all of which may be apparent. Violent shivering is another early sign, although this may cease as the condition develops.
- Stop and prevent further heat loss by providing shelter (lee of wall, boulder, survival bag) and adding insulation (spare clothes, sit-mat, sleeping-bag).
- Supply extra warmth with food, warm drink (*not* alcohol) and your own body heat by climbing into survival bag alongside the victim. Do *not* rub the skin to encourage circulation as this will further reduce core temperature.
- Prepare to move if the condition improves. If it does not, make the victim lie curled up in a slightly head down attitude and continue providing protection until the condition does improve.
- When ready, descend by the quickest and most sheltered route practical; but be fully prepared to stop again and repeat the procedure if the victim's condition deteriorates.
- If possible, send someone ahead to alert the mountain rescue.

Note Never assume death in an unconscious hypothermia victim, but continue treatment until expert help arrives.

Injury

Most injuries sustained while walking or scrambling come under one of three headings: minor sprains, fractures or dislocations caused by stumbling on rough ground; isolated but serious injuries caused by stonefall, ice-axes, and so on; and multiple injuries suffered during longer falls while scrambling or winter walking.

What sets these injuries apart from those sustained in everyday life is the delay before proper treatment can be administered; three or four hours may elapse before the casualty arrives at hospital. While no one would expect comprehensive medical treatment from a companion or passer-by, it falls to each of us to do what we can to stabilise the casualty's condition during that time.

Most accidents take place in bad weather and at the end of the day. Darkness soon closes in on the subdued group of people as they huddle together for warmth, exchanging nervous glances between themselves but avoiding the stare of the groaning bundle in their midst. Already it will be cold, wet and windy. An hour, maybe two, has passed since the messenger was sent to alert the rescue. The wait seems interminable. People are naturally resilient, often making complete recoveries from what seemed at the time to be horrific injuries, but their chances of survival depend heavily on the quality of care received during those first few hours; care which consists of basic treatment, comfort, warmth and reassurance (*see* First-aid Checklist).

- Protect the casualty from wind.
- Insulate with spare clothes and foam sit-mats.
- Leave a torch and whistle for the casualty to signal an approaching rescue team.
- Mark the site with cairns and make a mental note of nearby landmarks (take a compass bearing from one of them if necessary).
- Consider anchoring the casualty to the ledge to prevent another fall or delirious wanderings.

For urgent evacuations helicopters are frequently used. Usually, someone from the rescue team will be at hand to take charge and to advise bystanders of what to do before its approach. It could happen, however, that your first encounter is with the winchman at the end of his wire, in which case there are standard precautions to follow. These are given in the checklist.

16 Mountain Photography

Taking pictures adds interest to the day and texture to its recollection. The choice of equipment and technique depends very much on how the finished photographs will be viewed: in a snapshot album; on screen during a slide show; or in the pages of a magazine. Logically we begin with the choice of film.

FILM AND FORMAT

The supporting literature of mountaineering continually bombards us with photographs, and we have become discerning viewers. That being the case, the quality of our own results from small film formats, such as disc, 110 and half-frame, will be disappointing. The larger the film size, the better the quality; but medium and large format camera equipment is poorly adapted for use in the mountains. It is no surprise, then, that both casual and keen mountain photographers invariably choose the versatile 35mm format.

Too readily we dismiss colour print film as the stuff of snapshooters, but often that is precisely what we want – a personal record of the day's exploits. Although colour print film is an unsuitable medium for lecture shows and publication, it is by far the most convenient form of compiling a visual diary. Film of average speed (ISO100–200) retains adequate quality without losing the capacity to cope with occasionally unhelpful lighting conditions.

Colour transparency film remains popular among hill walkers, even though nowadays it is largely ignored by the general public. Without doubt, mountain views are portrayed most dramatically on the large scale of a projection screen – provided you can come to terms with the inconvenience. Professionals must use these films in preference to colour print because of lecturing and publication requirements. Pre-paid Kodachrome 64 gives very good results, whereas unavoidably long shutter speeds limit hand-held opportunities with the slower ISO25 version. Faster films (ISO200–400) are more versatile but lack fine quality. There is little room for error when exposing colour transparency film, and it is worth remembering that fully automatic cameras are ill-equipped for the fine adjustments required to compensate for non-average lighting conditions.

Black and white film has no worthwhile application unless you have access to a darkroom. Medium speed ISO125 film is the usual choice, whereas those interested in landscapes (and prepared to carry a tripod) will prefer the very slow films (ISO32–50). Fast film (ISO400) has limited application other than for hand-held telephoto shots, although variable speed films such as Ilford XP1 (ISO50–1600) offer tremendous latitude in awkward light.

CAMERAS

Camera choice within the 35mm format falls between compact and SLR, each representing a very different approach to photography. The first point to clarify is

The most useful zoom range includes the focal lengths 28–50, as opposed to the more conventional 35–70. Although specification of wide range zooms (35–135, 28–200, and so on) may look attractive on paper, cumbersome handling and variable image quality undermines their actual versatility. The fact that longer focal lengths are used relatively infrequently merely reinforces the argument.

Having gone to all the trouble of carrying an SLR system, many photographers will want to optimise quality by using fixed focal length lenses. The selection depends entirely on your field of interest, although as a rough guide it is wise to regard 35mm (as opposed to 50mm) as being the 'standard' lens. The majority of subjects will respond best to a wide rather than telephoto treatment, so you may decide to cater for the longer focal lengths in a zoom. In this case a concise lens selection for general purposes might be as follows: 24mm wide angle, 35mm standard, 70–210mm telephoto zoom. Sometimes an ultra-wide angle lens can be effective for getting in extra foreground or pulling down a dramatic sky, and a 20mm or even 17mm will find frequent application. Those interested in the world at their feet will want a lens with close focusing facility.

Camera Accessories

Few compact cameras have the facility for attaching filters or other accessories, so apart from spare film and batteries there is nothing else to carry. Conversely, owners of rangefinder or SLR cameras are presented with a bewildering array of additional equipment.

A wise precaution is to fit skylight filters and lens hoods to each lens. The filter protects the lens from scratches and cuts out some of the unwanted ultraviolet light, while the lens hood helps limit the occurrence of internal flare (which reduces contrast). A polarising filter will intensify colours in an otherwise pallid scene (especially limp blue skies), whereas a medium orange will do a similar job in monochrome. Other useful filters for black and white film are yellow/green, which lightens grass and gently darkens blue sky, and red, which strongly darkens blue sky.

The range of special effects filters for use with colour film is staggering. Most, however, are totally inappropriate in this context and are not worth bothering with. More useful are colour balancing filters which have a comparatively subtle influence on the result. A slightly warm filter will ease the blue cast encountered at altitude, while a neutral graduated filter will improve colour saturation in skies without excessively darkening the foreground.

Few other accessories are required, unless you have a special interest such as nature photography. Of these a tripod would bring about the single biggest improvement to picture quality. This is because a slow film, combined with a strong filter and long-focus lens, will bring shutter speeds perilously close to the hand-held limit – even on a bright summer's day. Lightweight tripods weighing around 1kg may be snubbed by 'pros' but provide adequate stability when used at their minimum extension. Besides, you will be tempted to leave behind a heavier model. Table-top tripods offer an even lighter and more compact platform, albeit at the expense of versatile head movements and proper support for long lenses.

*Fig 139 A padded waist pouch fits conveniently on to a rucksack
waistbelt, and the camera is always accessible.*

CARRYING THE CAMERA
(Fig 139)

Strange as it may seem, the camera case is almost as important as the camera itself. Good photographs will be missed unless the camera can be quickly brought to readiness. A rucksack lid pocket, for instance, cannot be regarded as accessible, nor can a so-called ever-ready case, which never is. By far the most convenient place for a compact camera is in a padded pouch fitted to a rucksack waistbelt or place of equal accessibility. These pouches, whether closed by zip or Velcro, are custom-made to fit most makes of compact camera. Photographic shops rarely stock them, although a large outdoor retailer will carry a reasonable selection.

SLR cameras pose more of a problem.

John Cleare (the prolific mountain photographer) maintains that any camera protection at all is a hindrance, preferring instead to carry his cameras clipped directly to rucksack shoulder pads. Most dare not take such risks with expensive equipment and compromise with a waist pack. When needed, this is swivelled to the front and unzipped to reveal camera and lens compartments. The problem with this kind of bag is that it fouls the rucksack. The major bag makers have produced special photo packs in an attempt to combat this difficulty. These fit like ordinary rucksacks but are compartmented to accept a comprehensive camera system (in addition to normal hill walking equipment). Unfortunately the packs are prohibitively expensive, and it may be worth experimenting with a daysack conversion.

151

Fig 140   *Placing the subject in its context. Evening on Crib*
Goch, photographed with a simple compact camera.

Fig 141   *Adding depth to the composition. Including a foreground*
feature often balances the composition and helps to
maintain the 3-D illusion (Loch Etive).

Fig 142   It is hard to go wrong with this pretty view of Blea
Tarn and the Langdale Pikes . . .

Fig 143   . . . but partial enlargement (equivalent to using a zoom
lens) simplifies and strengthens the composition without
losing any of the essential ingredients.

153

TAKING PICTURES
(Figs 140 to 143)

Enthusiasts will already have a fairly clear idea of the kind of pictures they want and how best to take them, so this section is directed more towards those exploring mountain photography for the first time.

Given that you are capable of loading a film and pressing the shutter release, your worst mistake would be to look only for the sort of subjects you think a 'proper' photographer would take. You'll be disappointed. The truly valuable shots are rarely the classically composed landscapes or even the moody sunsets, but simply the unpretentious pictures of you and your companions enjoying a day on the hills.

Having said that, you will want to place your subject in context. Apart from summit shots and other special moments (which are best snapped without delay so as not to lose the feel of the occasion), this means balancing the composition between the subject and its setting. Avoid the 'say cheese' full frontals if you can, but equally resist posing your subject too often in the 'land ahoy' type of rear view. Something between the two works best, so the moment when your companion pauses – perhaps to consult the map – is as good a time as any to take the shot.

Naturally you will want to vary the photographic record by including some competent views. Good composition is a subjective notion (if it looks good then it is good), but if there is one common factor among pleasing mountain photographs it is depth. That means filling the foreground with interesting shapes – pools, boulders, streams – anything, in fact, which will both contrast and complement the more distant view of the hills.

If you want to include a few evocative shots then all you have to do is ignore advice about never taking photos into the sun. Look sunwards for a simple composition – perhaps a figure or distinctive rock feature set against the sky – and simply let the camera work out the exposure for itself. It will get it 'wrong', automatically producing a moody semi-silhouette. The technique is particularly effective with snow scenes. Try it!

Appendix

USEFUL ADDRESSES

Association of British Mountain Guides
Private guiding and instruction. Contact
through the BMC.

Backpackers Club
The National Organising Secretary
20 St Michael's Road
Reading
Berkshire

Enclose a 9in by 4in s.a.e.

British Mountaineering Council (BMC)
Crawford House
Precinct Centre
Booth Street East
Manchester M13 9RZ
Courses, publications, access, insurance,
and so on. This is the best single source of
information and addresses.

Cicerone Press
Harmony Hall
Milnthorpe
Cumbria LA7 7QE
Publishers and distributors of walking and
scrambling guides and technical handbooks.

Cordee Books
3a De Montfort Street
Leicester LE1 7HD
Main distributors of UK and foreign maps,
guides, technical handbooks and narratives
on mountaineering subjects.

Glenmore Lodge
National Outdoor Training Centre
Aviemore PH22 1QU

Long Distance Walkers Association
Membership Secretary
Lodgefield Cottage
High Street
Flimwell
East Sussex

Enclose s.a.e.

Mountaineering Council of Scotland
15 Dowiesmill Lane
Edinburgh EH4 6DW

National Trust
42 Queen Anne's Gate
London SW1

Ordnance Survey
Romsey Road
Maybush
Southampton SO9 4DH

Map publishers and special mapping
services.

Plas y Brenin
National Centre for Mountain Activities
Capel Curig
Betws y Coed
Gwynedd LL24 OET

Ramblers' Association
1-5 Wandsworth Road
London SW8 2XX

Youth Hostels Association
Trevelyan House
8 St Stephens Hill
St Albans
Hertfordshire A11 2DY

SELECTED BIBLIOGRAPHY

Maps and Guidebooks

Ordnance Survey Maps

Landranger Series   General purpose maps at 1:50,000 scale for all areas.

Outdoor Leisure Series   1:25,000 scale maps (based on Pathfinder Series) of popular upland areas with additional information for visitors.

Pathfinder Series   Detailed maps at 1:25,000 scale and convenient size; excellent for route finding.

Tourist Maps   Convenient 1 inch to 1 mile maps of popular mountain areas. Effective use of shading. Good for basic route planning.

Scotland

Parker, J.W., *Scrambles in Skye* (Cicerone Press, 1983). Pocket guide in plastic covers to rock scrambles. Includes special large scale map.

Poucher, W.A., *Scottish Peaks* (Constable, 1965). Photo illustrated hardback guide to selected walks.

Scottish Mountaineering Trust, *The Munros* (SMT, 1985). Colour illustrated hardback guide/narrative to peaks over 3000 feet.

Small, A.D. (ed.), Scottish Mountaineering Club *District Guidebooks* (7 vols) (SMT, 1970). Illustrated hardback guides to mountain areas.

Williams, Noel, *Scrambles in Lochaber* (Cicerone Press, 1984). Pocket guide in plastic covers to rock scrambles in the Ben Nevis/Glencoe region.

Lake District

Evans, R.B., *Scrambles in the Lake District* 2nd edition (Cicerone Press, 1985). Pocket guide in plastic covers to selected rock and gill scrambles.

Poucher, W.A., *Lakeland Peaks* (Constable, 1960). Photo guide in hardback to some popular walks.

Wainright, A., *A Pictorial Guide to the Lakeland Fells* (8 vols) (Westmorland Gazette, 1955). Comprehensive and collectable walks guides illustrated with pen and ink drawings.

Wales

Ashton, Steve, *The Ridges of Snowdonia* (Cicerone Press, 1985). Illustrated guide/narrative in plastic covers to classic ridge walks.

Ashton, Steve, *Scrambles in Snowdonia* (Cicerone Press, 1980). Plastic-backed pocket guide to selected rock scrambles.

Marsh, Terry, *The Mountains of Wales* (Hodder & Stoughton, 1985). Illustrated paperback guide to selected walks.

Poucher, W.A., *Welsh Peaks* (Constable, 1962). Photo guide in hardback to some popular walks.

Technical Books

Barton, Bob, *A Chance in a Million* (SMT, 1985). The Scottish avalanche risk. Includes case histories.

British Mountaineering Council, *Mountain Hypothermia* (BMC, 1972). Concise leaflet, free from BMC office.

Cliff, Peter, *Mountain Navigation* 2nd edition (Cliff/Cordee Books, 1980). Concise paperback to essential techniques.

La Chappel, E., *ABC Avalanche Safety*

(Cordee Books). Inexpensive paperback.

Langmuir, Eric, *Mountaincraft and Leadership* (Scottish Sports Council and MLTB, 1984). Substantial handbook for hill walking group leaders.

March, Bill, *Modern Rope Techniques,* 3rd edition (Cicerone Press, 1985). Intricacies of ropework and improvised rescue. Paperback.

March, Bill, *Modern Snow & Ice Techniques,* 2nd edition (Cicerone Press, 1984). Basic and advanced techniques. Paperback.

Pedgley, David, *Mountain Weather* (Cicerone Press, 1979). Practical paperback guide to weather conditions most often encountered in the hills.

Renouf, J. & Hulse, S., *First Aid for Hillwalkers & Climbers* (Cicerone Press, 1982). Convenient paperback manual.

Wilson, J.G., *Follow the map* (A&C Black and Ordnance Survey, 1985). All about maps.

General Reading

Butterfield, I., *The High Mountains of Britain and Ireland* (Diadem, 1986): Substantial illustrated hardback guide/narrative to walks.

Gilbert, R. & Wilson, K., *Big Walks* (Diadem, 1980). Large format illustrated guide/narrative to demanding UK walks and scrambles.

Gilbert, R. & Wilson, K., *Classic Walks* (Diadem, 1981). Companion volume to *Big Walks* with less ambitious selection.

Magazines

Climber   Hill walking, scrambling, climbing.

High   Hill walking, scrambling, climbing.

Mountain   Climbing, mountaineering.

The Great Outdoors   Rambling, backpacking, hill walking.

METRIC CONVERSIONS

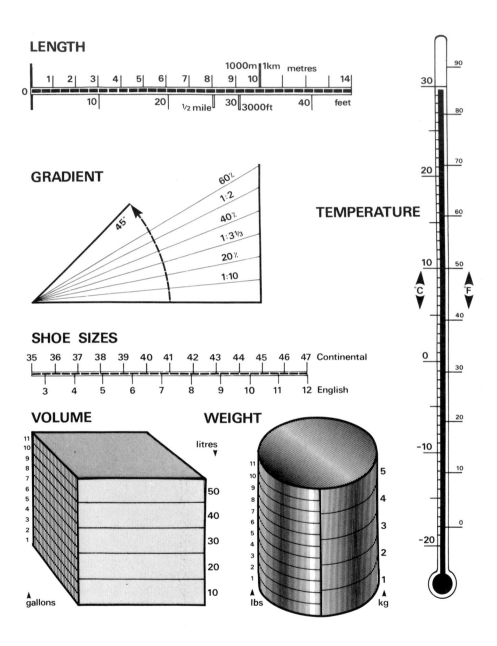

LENGTH

metres: 1 2 3 4 5 6 7 8 9 10 1000m 1km 14

feet: 10 20 ½ mile 30 3000ft 40

GRADIENT

45°
60%
1:2
40%
1:3⅓
20%
1:10

SHOE SIZES

Continental: 35 36 37 38 39 40 41 42 43 44 45 46 47

English: 3 4 5 6 7 8 9 10 11 12

VOLUME

litres: 50 40 30 20 10
gallons: 11 10 9 8 7 6 5 4 3 2 1

WEIGHT

kg: 5 4 3 2 1
lbs: 11 10 9 8 7 6 5 4 3 2 1

TEMPERATURE

°C: 30 20 10 0 -10 -20
°F: 90 80 70 60 50 40 30 20 10 0

Index